RAYZOR'S EDGE

ROB RAY'S TOUGH LIFE ON THE ICE

Rob Ray
with Budd Bailey

SportsPublishingLLC.com

ISBN 13: 978-1-59670-283-7

Publishers: Peter L. Bannon and Joseph J. Bannon Sr.
Senior managing editor: Susan M. Moyer
Acquisitions editor: John Humenik
Developmental editor: Doug Hoepker
Art director: Dustin J. Hubbart
Dust jacket design: Dustin J. Hubbart
Interior layout: Rachel E. Hubbart
Photo editor: Jessica Martinich

Sports Publishing L.L.C.
804 North Neil Street
Champaign, IL 61820
Phone: 1-877-424-2665
Fax: 217-363-2073
www.SportsPublishingLLC.com

Printed in the United States of America

CIP Data available upon request.

To Juliean and Jody

CONTENTS

FOREWORD
BY MATTHEW BARNABY

My first encounter with Rob Ray came in 1992 when I was 19 and coming into my first professional training camp with the Buffalo Sabres. Obviously, I was very nervous going to camp in the first place. I was trying to make the team as a "tough guy" at that point, and Rob was the tough guy there. I remember walking into the dressing room, wanting to see how we compared in terms of physical size.

I was a little uncomfortable around him at first because of who he was. I wasn't even done with junior hockey then, and I had grown up watching NHL players. Rob wasn't that much older than I was at the time—five years—but it seemed like a lot. I was like a kid at that point, and he was someone I looked up to.

I played a little in Buffalo for the next few seasons, while Rob and I were vying for the same job. He was the heavyweight, and he was much, much tougher than I ever was. I don't think it was until I made the team full time in 1995 that we really became close friends. Rob is a very guarded person. Until you get to know him, you don't really appreciate him. He was there to help me do all sorts of things—getting a place to live, getting accustomed to the life, telling me to save my money because it wouldn't last forever. I also learned a lot by watching the way he worked with charities. He helped me with every little aspect of the game that comes with playing in the National Hockey League.

If someone meets Rob Ray for the first time, they aren't sure how to take him. That's the way he is. He doesn't let a lot of people "in" at first glance. He wants to check them out. He analyzes people. In this job, there are a lot of people who want a lot of different things. Rob is very good at letting good people into his life. Once that happens, though, Rob will do anything for anyone. If I called Rob right now and told him I needed him to drive to Texas to see me about something, I know he'd get in the car and do it. And he'd do it for a lot of different people. That's the type of person he is. I've played with hundreds of players in my 14 years as a pro. Rob is the only guy that I remain close to. That says a lot about him as a person, and what he's done for me.

Rob and I played on some interesting teams with the Sabres, and we were caught up in all sorts of situations. When times were tough during Rob's time in Buffalo, he was the visible face of the Sabres. He gave people someone to root for when there wasn't much going on with the team.

In this book, you'll get to meet Rob, the most animated Sabre of all time. You're going to find out what was in his mind while he was wearing a Buffalo sweater. We all watched him play, and noted his antics. But this book is your chance to get to know the *real* Rob Ray. I guarantee you, speaking as an ex-teammate and as a friend, you're going to learn a lot, because if Rob is one thing, it's brutally honest.

1

THE ENFORCER

I used to punch people for a living.

I also skated and shot and passed and checked and helped young players on and off the ice and did a bunch of other things. It was all part of my role as an enforcer in the National Hockey League. It's just that the part that involved fighting was the one that turned up on the television highlights.

You'd be surprised how many people didn't understand my role. They didn't "get it." Too many people looked at me and said, "You're not a good player because you don't score goals and get assists every night." But those were the people who didn't understand the game and probably still don't. They have to learn that intangibles don't get printed on the scoresheet. Hitting a guy, holding him up, delivering a hit to change the momentum of the game, or drawing a penalty so my team could score a goal—there's much more to hockey than some people think.

Even some of my own teammates didn't completely understand what guys like me around pro hockey did. We had an argument in practice once because somebody put money up to give to the guy who scored the winning goal in a particular game.

"Why would you give it to him only?" I asked. "There will be four other guys on the ice, plus a goalie. He won't get the opportunity without those other guys helping him." There's a great deal that happens before someone scores a game-winning goal, and guys who play like I did are a part of it.

I have heard a lot of people over the years say things like, "Rob is a bad man because he beats people up for a living." I have tried to explain to them that the fighting was part of my job. That was what the team expected me to do. I wanted to stand before the fans as a good role model. Maybe that's one of the reasons why I did, and still do, so many charitable functions off the ice. Those people who say I was a "bad man" are ignorant about hockey because they don't know the whole situation. It wasn't my job to be their child's role model when I was playing. I can be a hero or idol, but it's the parents' job to teach right from wrong.

It seems like I was always trying to defend myself and my behavior. With the Bills, if a lineman makes a great block to let the quarterback make a great play, he usually doesn't get much credit for it. The quarterback gets the credit. Meanwhile, the lineman's stopped three guys. It's like that in hockey. If I could affect a game and allow our top players to score at key times or prevent an important goal, I did my job.

My role on the team was much more difficult than you might think. Many of my teammates looked at what I did and said, "I would never want your job." And there were days where I couldn't hang on to my stick because my hands were so sore. I bobbled passes and had trouble shooting the puck, but the guys wouldn't give me a hard time about it. Most of them knew not to say a word, because they understood. When I did something good, they were the first ones to congratulate and encourage me.

Too many casual hockey fans look at fights and think players are "rassling," that they stage all their fights. Those fights are very real, and I've got the scars to prove it. In 1995 I broke the orbital bone under my eye. Tony Twist of the Blues hit me in a fight in St. Louis, and my whole head felt like it instantly went hollow. Some air under my skin went down into my cheek, hit my jaw, and then came back up my face as a bubble. Everyone in the dressing room was watching it. When the air pocket hit my eye, the eye shut, and I couldn't pry it open for seven days. I had to wait until the air worked itself out.

I have a plate with five screws in my thumb from the time I fought Steve Webb of the Islanders in 1997 and tried to give him an uppercut. I didn't get my hand turned in time, and I broke my thumb.

I broke my knuckles fighting against Ottawa's Dennis Vial in 1994. I had my jaw broken, and all the disks in my jaw are gone. Some days my jaw locks. I've got arthritis in both my elbows. I got hit in the chest once, and my rib popped out of its place. The cartilage broke, leaving my rib exposed. I got taped up, but it didn't help much. I couldn't shoot the puck. There was nothing the doctors could do. They said if I wanted to take the time to let it heal, fine. But otherwise, I just had to deal with the pain … which I did.

Plus, there are the million little aches and pains that I accumulated in 955 games in the National Hockey League. There were days when I sat at home and waited for the Advil to kick in so I could use my hands to drive to the arena. You may hear stories about guys like me being in more pain under certain weather conditions. Well, that's real—and it hurts. People don't see that.

There was no preventing the things that happened on the ice. And they will all catch up to me in the future. I didn't think about injuries when I got them. Maybe an hour after an incident, when I had gotten blurred vision or a mild concussion or something, I wondered, "Is this ever going to go away? Will I be messed up down the road?"

I try to hope that medical technology will have improved enough in the future so that they'll be able to fix me up when I'm older. I don't care if you play sports or not—everyone will have to deal with some of those aches and pains. To me, the benefits of playing sports outweighed any medical problems I might have down the road. I was lucky enough to play at a time when guys who play several years in this league should be set for life. There are guys who aren't, of course, but I hope I'll be fine.

At least medical care from the team has improved over the years. The staff doesn't let guys play after they are really hurt. Years ago, too many guys were shot up and frozen, which led to more severe injuries. That doesn't happen so often anymore.

I've taken shots and pills. I wanted to play, although I asked questions before I received any medical treatment. If the doctors said I wouldn't do any permanent damage by taking a shot, so be it—"Let's go." I had a job to do.

***

Many people think I was always an enforcer, but that is hardly the case. I've been playing hockey for almost as long as I've been able to stand up, and I used to be one of those big scorers. From Day One I got a lot of attention. I was on my first team at three, my first travel team at five. I got to play before the other kids because I could skate. I was always on the power play and was always one of the team's top scorers and one of the best skaters on the team. That was all true right up until the time I played junior hockey. Heck, I was a 14-year-old defenseman in my last season of mite hockey.

When I was 15, I played Junior B hockey in Trenton in the 1983-84 season. That's when I was playing with 20-year-olds for the first time. I looked around and said, "Wow, there's a big difference here. I'm a child, and those guys are men." Twenty isn't that old, but there's quite a difference between 15 and 20. That really opened my eyes to that fact that there's a lot more to the game of hockey than scoring every night. I started to learn how to do more than score goals at that age. That year, I didn't play all the time, but at least I was on the team. I had 11 goals in 40 games with only 57 penalty minutes. I thought then that if I didn't go any further in hockey, I still would have had a great time playing the game.

The next year, I played a lot on an expansion team in Tier II Junior A called the Whitby Lawmen. Teppo Numminen, a Sabre defenseman for the last couple of years, was on that team. I was a young guy—16. The owners were trying to promote the team, and I helped give it an image. I was feisty. That year I got a lot of penalty minutes—318. There were fights, but it was really closer to wrestling. There was a lot of stuff that went on in those leagues. But I still didn't have the role I had with the Sabres.

From there I went to junior hockey—the Cornwall Royals of the Ontario Hockey League—in 1985, and my role changed some more. I was expected to be part of the offense because there was less fighting. But I was also expected to be a good defensive player and a grinder. It took me a couple of years to play regularly there. It was tough; I didn't really have anyone who'd talk to me about my situation. We were just expected to do our job, whatever it was, and that was it. "We're giving you an opportunity, and it's up to you to take advantage of it" was the attitude.

I think that made me mentally tough. When I came to the

Buffalo organization and the coaches told me to change my game in order to reach the NHL, I knew I could do it. I had done it before, so I could do it again.

I had some penalty minutes in Cornwall, but I could score too. I had 11 goals and 41 assists for 52 points (with 179 penalty minutes) in 61 games my last junior season in 1987-88. There were guys who were considered the league's best fighters, but some of them could play too. Shayne Corson was a tough guy. Brendan Shanahan was considered a big fighter back then. There were other tough guys in the OHL who were scary but who never really made it any higher up the ladder.

When I came to Rochester for the 1988-89 season, head coach John Van Boxmeer came to me and said, "This is what you've got to do to reach the NHL." Boxy told me I had to learn how to be an enforcer, and that to make the NHL I needed to take Kevin Maguire and Mike Hartman's job.

He never had to tell me again. The coaches aren't always going to put their arms around players and tell them what to do. Players have to know that. The coaches treat you like a man by that point, and you have to act like one and know what to expect. I had 446 penalty minutes in my only full year (1988-89) in the minors, and had 335 penalty minutes for the Amerks in only 43 games the next season.

There were a few guys on those teams who were in the minors for a couple of years, and then I never saw them again. They didn't do what was expected of them. The team's attitude was, "If you aren't going to do it, there are other guys out there who will." Joel Savage and Darcy Loewen were top draft choices of the Sabres, but they didn't do their jobs. They were out of hockey by the mid-1990s. Meanwhile, a guy like Donald Audette, who played with me in

Rochester, was expected to score. Donald did whatever it took to score goals, because that was his job. He was like that throughout his career. We both played for a long time in the NHL because we did our jobs.

If you talk to the guys in the NHL who have filled the enforcer's role for an extended period of time and been successful at it, there's not one of them who will say they had things handed to them coming up through hockey. They were never overly skilled players. They all will say they had to earn their position. They all will say it's tough to sit there for long periods of time and then be tapped on the shoulder and told to go fight. And if you didn't do it, you were done.

There was added pressure because players had to say, "I've got to fight tonight." There's a level of respect among players in general in that role. We know what it took for enforcers to get there. It's different for offensive players. Sure they can score goals. Big deal. Anyone can score a goal eventually. We know the physical players bust their rears. They are never given much credit.

Enforcers are the ones who can get upset because they have to protect some guy who makes $7 million. Players ask, "Why do I have to go look after that guy?" The answer is: "Because it's your job."

Enforcers don't receive a great deal of playing time. It was difficult to adjust to that, especially when I was a rookie. I remember sitting there, getting one shift a game—there were 11 games in my career when I didn't even get on the ice—and I started questioning myself. "What's wrong with me?" I asked. I had to hold back tears on the bench because I thought I was doing something wrong. I thought I'd be in Rochester to play in the minors the next day, or not be in the lineup for the next game. Almost every day of my career, I was a little worried whether I was going to be in the lineup.

I never had a stretch in my career when I could say, "I'm playing tomorrow." I never had the chance to get comfortable.

I did get used to a limited amount of playing time, but some nights it was still tough to just sit there. It almost becomes a matter of pride. I'd be sitting on the bench, yapping at someone, and the answer would come back, "You haven't been on the ice yet." I just had to say, "You got me."

***

Hockey fights follow certain patterns. They start when the two players are fresh, preferably right at the beginning of a shift. If somebody gets hurt, the other guy stops punching. Why go any longer? He's done his job. If someone goes down to the ice, the fight is over. If I had a guy tied up and he was bleeding badly, I'd say, "You're cut." If he wanted to keep going, fine. Otherwise, we stopped.

I see guys who aren't fighters who will wrestle when they hit the ground. When it was over with me, I just wanted to let go of the jersey and get to the penalty box.

One time, Tie Domi and I got into a fight where both of us just threw punches. We threw and threw and threw. Then we looked at each other and we both thought, "Is that enough?" We stopped right there. We'd proved our point.

I had boxing lessons when I was younger. That gave me a few pointers that helped throughout my career. I learned how to throw a punch. A lot of guys just use their arms or shoulders. If you watch a boxer, you'll notice that they punch from the hip. It gives them more power. I learned how to block a punch and how to deflect a punch with the off-arm. I learned how to throw an uppercut and set up that punch after throwing a couple at the head. It's just little techniques. The guys who know how to throw a punch are the guys who hurt other players.

Most guys study the other team's fighters. Are they lefties? Do they stand and throw them? But after a while in the league, I fought guys enough times to know what they'd do.

I didn't want to be the guy who lunged right in, so sometimes I circled and circled. The guys who make the first move in a fight sometimes can get really popped. When players get angry, they just come right in at you, and that's what you want. The guy who lunges is not thinking about what he's doing. He's going more on aggression than anything else. The young guys will do that more than the veterans. You just sack them when they get there.

I used to be famous around the league for having my shirt come off during fights. At one time I wasn't as big as the guys I fought against, so I had to come up with a trick to compensate. In any fight, the first thing the other guy tries to do is grab a jersey so he can get some balance, get set, and start throwing. I decided if my jersey wasn't there, he'd have nothing to hang on to. I would go on the offense while he hung on. I didn't tie my shoulder pads on, so I'd duck when he grabbed my jersey, and everything came right off. Then he would stand there with a jersey in his hand, and I'd go after him.

That worked for me. It worked for a long enough period of time that it gave me confidence. Then in 1996 the NHL passed a rule to prevent jersey removal during fights. Sure enough, the media called it "The Rob Ray Rule." When the league put the rule in, it took me a while to get that confidence back. When I got older and a little smarter, it didn't bother me.

I really didn't fight that many different guys over the years, but it's funny how many different uniforms they wore. Enforcers usually bounce from team to team. I was an exception, starting my career in Buffalo and staying there for more than a decade until I played parts of two seasons in Ottawa.

Domi played in Toronto for a while, but he also played in Winnipeg and New York before returning to the Maple Leafs. Craig Berube played for Washington, Toronto, Calgary, Philadelphia, and the New York Islanders. Almost every veteran enforcer moves all the time.

As long as I did my job, I wasn't going to get in trouble. I wasn't going to be the guy who had a finger pointed at him. I was always afraid of being a scapegoat, so I always tried to do what I was supposed to do and, hopefully, a little more.

And I did that job for 14 seasons with the Sabres. Not many guys are with the same team for that long—that feat will become even more rare in the years to come. With free agency, guys will go where the money is. During the last two times I went through unrestricted free agency when I was a regular, I was offered more money to play in other cities. It would have been nice to make more money, but when I sat down and thought about moving expenses, paying more in taxes, and so forth, in the long run it wasn't worth it to give up what I had in Buffalo. Besides, I'd probably have been a lesser player in another city. I wouldn't have had enough time to rebuild that comfort zone. All that time with the Sabres made me very easy to please. I didn't go into games thinking about hat tricks. I had lower goals toward the end of my career.

One time, I was talking to Dave Andreychuk, my linemate. "Let's go score a goal. I don't care if I get a point. I want a plus," I told him.

"You're happy with the plus?" he asked.

"I'm happy with the plus. I don't care who gets it. Let's score. As long as I'm a part of it."

I may not have played as much as the other guys, but at least I was part of the team. I'd rather have sat on the bench than watched from the stands. I did what I loved to do. When the coach told me to go, I went—for one shift or a thousand.

2

MY GREATEST HITS

If you search for my name on one of those Internet auction sites, you'll find the usual hockey cards and autographed pictures. You'll also find the odd fight tape or DVD. There are some videos put out by the NHL in which I pop up occasionally, and there are others put together by amateurs with nothing but my fights on it.

It's kind of fun to watch them every once in a while. And sometimes my buddies will come over and watch them with me. It's not like I look at them and say, "This is my highlight reel," but I still remember all of the fights.

When I see some of them now, I realize why I had trouble defending myself at first. I had to learn not to go into it so gung-ho, and not fight as much. I used to just throw myself into a fight without thinking—just grab on and go and go and go. I learned to take a couple just to give a couple.

So have a seat, and I'll take you through some memorable fights, incidents, and personalities.

ED BELFOUR

We were playing in Chicago one night, and Pat LaFontaine

crashed into Blackhawks goalie Ed Belfour. Everyone piled up, including me.

Well, Patty crawled underneath the pile. He had his gloves on his hands and said, "Rayzor, put your head in between my gloves so they can't hit you."

The line on the ice for that incident was LaFontaine-Ray-Alexander Mogilny. There wasn't too much help for me there when problems started.

DAVE BROWN

I had a fight with him a couple of years into my career that really helped my confidence.

Philadelphia's Brown was a big guy—6-5, 222. We went at it for quite a while. Toward the end, I caught him with a really solid punch, and he grabbed on to me and said something like, "Eeeehhh." I can tell when I've hit someone hard. I can hear the wind come right out of them.

That really turned me around mentally. I felt like I belonged in the league after that.

THE CALGARY BENCH

Sometimes a fight will start, and before you know it, you are over the boards and in their bench.

In December 1991, we played Calgary at home. It was the first game between the teams since LaFontaine had had his jaw broken when we played them in Calgary about three weeks before that. Grant Ledyard, a couple of other guys, and I wound up in their bench, fighting away.

That was when such incidents were "fun." If you did that now, you'd be in so much trouble you couldn't afford to play. You'd be broke.

You're really in enemy territory when you wind up on the other bench. I remember what happened when guys wound up on our bench while I was sitting there, and trust me—we started laying the skates to them, kicking them, giving them the end of the stick—anything we could do that nobody would see. That's not a fun place to be. I've been there.

Even when a fight is just by the bench rather than in it, guys give it to you verbally. It doesn't happen now as much as it used to, but back then guys always tried to get me going by talking trash. On the other hand, I loved giving it to guys when I was just sitting there, watching a fight.

DOWN ON THE FARM

When I signed with the Ottawa Senators in 2004, they sent me to their American Hockey League team in Binghamton for a week to get into shape. I hadn't played a game in nine months when I suited up for Binghamton for the first time, which was a game in Syracuse. This big kid came up and said, "We going to go?"

"Man, can you give me a period or two to warm up?" I said.

"What do you mean?"

"I haven't played in nine months. I just started skating hard last week. This is my first game. Can you give me a period to get into it?"

Then the puck dropped, and he said nope. He started beating on me right there. We fought and fought. The officials finally broke it up.

In Syracuse, the rink is about as big as a matchbox, but when I looked to see where the penalty box was after the fight, it looked like it was in Buffalo. I didn't think I was going to make it.

Another time in Springfield, some big young kid came up to me early in the game during a face-off. "Hey, legend, are we going to go?" he asked.

"What?" I answered.

"Are we going to go?"

"Do we have to? How about a stick instead? How about two sticks? They will be in your stall after the game."

"OK," and he took off.

TODD FEDORUK

We played the Flyers in November 2000, and before the game, as before all others, the coaches told us exactly who was playing—who they were and everything about them. If there were some new kids up, they let us know about them so we'd be prepared when we went out for the game. But nothing was ever said about Fedoruk, nothing about him ever having fought or anything. He hadn't even played in an NHL game before that season.

Fedoruk and I lined up next to each other for a face-off. All of a sudden he said, "Wanna go?"

I looked at him and said, "What?"

"You want to go?"

"Who are you?"

He looked at me and said, "Hey, I play just like you. I just got called up. You want to go?"

At this point, I thought he was trying to con me in to draw a penalty. So I said, "OK, we'll go." After the puck dropped I backed off just to see what he was going to do. Sure enough, he dropped his gloves. I said to myself, "All right, let's go."

We got in the fight. When it was over, I said, "Good fight." He was a young guy and everything, so I gave him a little boost of confidence.

"Thanks, man," he answered. "That was unbelievable. Unbelievable." And he took off for the penalty box.

After the period ended, he told the guys in his dressing room he was surprised I didn't know who he was. "Can you believe he never heard of me before? Can you believe that?" he said.

PAUL KRUSE

Here's a reason you learn not to carry many grudges in this business. I had a fight with Paul Kruse of the Islanders on March 10, 1998, in Long Island. Two weeks later, we traded Jason Dawe to the Islanders … for Kruse.

It happens a lot. I had some good scraps with Gord Donnelly, and then he became a Sabre. How many times did I go with Denny Vial? Lots, and then he turned up in our training camp one time.

We joke around about it. You have to put it behind you.

CHRIS NILAN

Chris Nilan was one of several tough guys on the Bruins when I first came to the league, like Lyndon Byers, Bob Sweeney, and Darin Kimble.

Back then we played seven or eight games against each team in the division, so we really got to know each other. It was funny to fight guys like Nilan. I grew up watching them on television, saying, "Boy, these guys are tough." It took a while for me to get over the sensation of being in awe of them.

I never wanted to be traded anywhere for most of my career, but if I had been forced to go somewhere, I think I would have fit in with the Bruins back then. But things aren't the same since they left Boston Garden.

The fans in Boston can be pretty funny. One time I skated around the ice during a TV break to get loose. When I came back to the bench, someone yelled, "Good shift!"

I got one of them back once, though. This guy was behind me and was just relentless with his verbal abuse. I couldn't even yell back at him, because the glass was so high. One of our equipment guys was standing behind me, so I said, "George, you got a marker?" He gave one to me. I took the blade on my stick, and wrote "800K" on the white tape of the blade. I gave the marker back and waited until the guy started screaming again. Then I held up the stick, pointed to it and then to myself, and shook my head up-and-down at him.

Everybody in that section loved it. The guy never even sat back down. He just went up the stairs and was gone. I peeled the tape off the stick and retaped it just in case I had to go back on the ice.

The money angle doesn't always work. One time the Sabres were in San Jose, and one fan was giving it to us. Someone on our bench yelled up, "He's making $1.3 million. What are you making?"

The guy said, "Hey, pal, this is the Silicon Valley. You've got to make at least $3 million before you're a somebody here."

It's not too often a fan says something that fast, but that guy buried us.

LYLE ODELEIN

One time in Montreal, I got caught near the Canadiens' bench. About three guys pushed me into the boards, and Odelein came over the top and threw punches at me. I had no chance to defend myself.

When something like that happens, the first thing that goes through your mind is "hide." You have to try to protect yourself and hope some help shows up.

A QUEBEC FAN

This is one that most people remember. It still pops up on ESPN's highlights when it does a segment on dumb fans.

The Sabres were playing in Quebec in 1992. There was a fight on the ice involving our goalie, Clint Malarchuk, and Herb Raglan of the Nordiques. Herbie went flying into Clint when Clint was playing the puck. Clint did a somersault in the air. It led to a five-on-five scrum on the ice.

We were all watching on the ice, and suddenly someone said, "What's going on?" We looked, and this guy was sitting on top of the glass near the bench.

John Muckler, our coach, yelled, "Give me a stick! I'll get him," and grabbed Ken Sutton's stick. Muckler ran down the bench, ready to hit the guy and knock him back over the glass. Just as Muckler went to hit him, the fan dove in front of the bench near the defensemen.

By that time, I was at the far end of the bench by the door, pushing everyone to get down to where the guy was. We grabbed onto him, wrestled around with him, and threw him out on the ice.

As soon as he hit the ice, he jumped back up and came running back at us, right where I was. I couldn't tell if he was drunk or anything, and I didn't know what he was going to do next. I grabbed him by the hair with my left hand, and his head was by the boards. I think I hit him 17 or 18 straight times. I stopped because my hand got so sore. The police were there by the end. When I let the guy go, I had a ball of black hair in my left hand, which I had pulled out of his head.

He fell on the ice. The two or three police officers jumped on him and wrestled around with him. Eventually the guy was handcuffed and taken off between the two benches. We still couldn't believe it.

Then when we looked out on the ice, we saw that one of the officer's belts had fallen, spilling bullets all over the ice. The stuff had to be picked up. We started playing a couple of minutes later, and everyone was still saying, "What just happened here?" That highlight made all of the networks that night.

A lot of things went through my mind when it took place. Does he have a weapon? Is he going to hurt somebody? I figured I had to protect my teammates from him; I thought it was my responsibility. I didn't know what was going to happen.

It cost me $7,000 in fines for straightening things out. The team paid for it, and then it was deducted from my salary. At that time I was young and didn't know any better. I guess I learned a lesson.

By the way, I've never gone into the stands after a fan or anything like that, although I've seen people swing sticks at fans a couple of times.

UNIDENTIFIED ENFORCER

I won't name the player, but the story is worth telling. We were on the road, and an enforcer on the other team was known for having girlfriends. He was dating one girl even though he was married to someone else.

One time during a stoppage of play, the guy looked in the stands, started banging on the glass and screamed, "Get away! Get away!" We couldn't figure out what was going on.

It turned out that the guy's girlfriend and the girlfriend's mother were at the game, and they were going to go up to his wife in the stands.

MICK VUKOTA

Mick and I squared off for years. He'd throw a few punches and then grab my leg and try to throw me down. It happened all the time. One time the laces to my pants came undone that way. I skated off the ice with my legs open so that my pants would stay up.

We had a couple of odd fights. One time in Buffalo, I talked some trash at Al Arbour, the Islanders coach—nothing out of the ordinary. Suddenly, Vukota came up to me and screamed, "You don't say that to Al!" We went at it, and both of us left the ice. He kept screaming when the two of us were in the hallway just in front of the locker room door, because the runways at the Aud weren't really that far apart. That sort of thing happened a lot there just because of the way the arena was set up. At least security people were there to make sure nothing else happened.

Then in April 1995, we played the Islanders in New York. We were ahead, 5–1, and there was less than eight minutes left. Both of us had been on the bench for just about the whole game. We both came out on the ice at the same time. He had a certain look in his face, and he said, "Are you as embarrassed as I am?"

"What are you talking about?" I said.

"We sat on the bench the whole game. Are you as embarrassed as I am?"

"Yeah, well, if you put it that way, yeah, I am."

"What do you say we just get out of here, then?"

"All right."

"But we can't stop. We have to get ten minutes so we can get thrown out."

We threw punches, and then we sort of wrestled around. We both got misconducts and were thrown out of the game. As soon it was over he said, "See ya."

3

GROWIN' UP

Stirling, Ontario, is exactly the kind of place you might picture if I told you I grew up in a small Ontario farm town. It's directly north of Rochester across Lake Ontario, about ten to 15 miles inland. If you're driving, it's about two and a half hours from Toronto, three and a half hours from Montreal, and 45 minutes southeast of Peterborough. When I grew up there in the 1970s, the sign at the edge of town said, "Stirling—1,200 people." Now there are 1,800 residents. The nicest building is probably the arena. It has hockey and curling, just like every other arena in a small town in Canada. Stirling has about seven churches, a rather large number for a town that size. I always went to church, and I was a regular at Sunday School until I was a teenager. Before my image is shattered, though, I should mention I was not an altar boy and I was not in the choir or anything.

It's a nice, clean town where everyone knows everybody. Stirling is in the middle of a beautiful area. Rawdon Creek runs right through the middle of it, and there are a lot of lakes nearby, so hunting and fishing are huge. A lot of people come in to camp in the summer.

The Rays have lived in Stirling forever. My father's name is John, and he owned a store until he retired in 2000. He had wanted to quit for a number of years so he could finally relax. My dad is a man who thought he had to be at the shop all the time. You know the type—he thought things wouldn't run unless he was there. The business was in our family for 58 years. My grandfather started it as a blacksmith shop. Then he started selling tractors, and the store graduated into farm machinery. The business was good for our family.

I worked at the store with my dad starting when I was 12 years old. Every summer for the next dozen years or so, I worked five days a week like everyone else. At the time I thought working there was awful, but the experience taught me discipline, respect, and appreciation for what I had.

I didn't stop working there until the 1994-95 hockey season, when I bought my own house in suburban Buffalo. Before that, I was making about $300,000 a year, and I still went home every summer, put in my five-day workweek, and took home a $200 check. I was expected to come back every year, and I felt like I was needed. I definitely figured when I was growing up that I would spend my life working at the shop. I felt that way even after the Sabres drafted me as a 20-year-old. I figured after I eventually left the NHL, I'd return to work at the shop, which my father also expected of me. Obviously, it didn't work out that way. I think my dad was a little disappointed about that at first, but now he knows that I had a long career and that everyone has benefited from it.

While my dad spent his whole life in Stirling, my mom, Edith, came to Ontario from Holland. She came over on a boat when she was six or seven with her mother, father, brother, and sister. She also had a brother born over here. When the family moved into Stirling, they lived about a thousand yards from my dad on Church Street. Mom's father—my grandpa—came over to my dad's house to do masonry work. That became the family business on that side of the family.

My mom used to work at a soda shop in town, and that's where my parents met. Eventually they got married and began living happily ever after.

I have one sister, Cindy, who is 14 months older than I am. We always had the typical brother-sister fights when we were growing up. I left home when I was 15, but my name still came up a lot once I started to play junior hockey. People were always talking about me and asking her about me. She was just "Rob Ray's sister" and not "Cindy Ray." That was hard on her. By the time I made it to the NHL, she was hundreds of miles away, having kids and living her life. We were never at the age where we could understand each other, be together, and have some fun.

It wasn't until after I'd been in Buffalo for a few years that Cindy and I worked it all out. We actually sat down and talked about it, and since then everything has been phenomenal. We're best friends. We talk all the time. I look forward to the phone calls, the e-mails, and the pictures. Cindy even turns to me when she's got problems.

Cindy and her husband, Dave, have two boys, Curtis and Zachary, and hockey is their life. I know the feeling. I don't remember not playing the game. I played on my first team at three. Our yard had the house and shop all on the same property. I used to walk across the street and go on to the frozen creek in the winter. We were always there. I played on my first travel team at five; the farthest trip may have been to Brighton, which was a 45-minute drive.

I was decent at hockey from the start, and I was a good skater. I scored a ton of goals every year. I could have scored a lot more. As my dad would say, "If you didn't put the puck into the goalie's pads, you'd score a lot more goals." Even then I had a good touch, but not a great touch.

When I was growing up, all I did was play hockey in the winter and softball in the summer. There was nothing else. And every kid played. In every age group, you'd have 12 to 15 guys show up for tryouts, so every kid made the team. I played against older kids a lot because the age group ahead of me often didn't have enough players. That really helped my development.

It's a good thing I had hockey, because otherwise I wouldn't have played with anyone when I was really little. I was a quiet kid, believe it or not. My mother always said that if she didn't know for sure that I was in the house, she'd never know I was around. I always played by myself quietly. I was never the center of attention and never had a lot of friends. I think I fit in at the arena well enough, but I had some problems with the other kids because of hockey. I was always the best player on the team from Day One. I think a lot of other kids who didn't play hockey weren't friendly because of that. Scoring all those goals made me different than the other kids; I wasn't one of the guys.

I was not a good student right from the time I was in kindergarten. In fact, I was awful. I stunk at reading and comprehension. I still can't spell, but I can't blame my parents for that. They always put school first. If I didn't do my homework, I didn't play hockey. Looking back, I think I just wasn't interested in studying. My mind drifted in school. It just seemed like I was interested in everything but studying. Once I got a little older, I did a little better at it. When I got to high school, I was the scholastic player of the year two out of three years, but I didn't enjoy being in school. I was sort of on the edge of the "in crowd." That was hard. Hockey was about the only thing I had in common with a lot of kids my own age. If I hadn't played sports, I never would have had many friends.

If you talk to anyone from Canada who is in the NHL, he'll tell you about how important his parents were in helping him along the way. It was no different for me. My parents were always there. But my dad wasn't a sports fan. I was told he was a pretty good hockey player when he was younger. I saw him play a few times in old-timers leagues and beer leagues, but I can't remember him playing much. He was so dedicated to work. It's funny, but we never even watched sports at home. There was the odd time when we'd watch *Hockey Night in Canada* on Saturday nights, and I think we watched the Grey Cup every year.

My dad came to my games when he could, but as soon as the game was over, he would go back to work. He was always interested in what I did and would talk about it, but he never pushed me. My hockey games were never a major event in my family when I was growing up, even though I was good at it. But my mom was always there, and dad was there quite a bit too.

When I needed hockey advice from a family member, I turned to my uncle Robert, my mom's youngest brother. He was an unbelievable player, the best player in our town when he was growing up. Robert had an opportunity to go to Europe to play, but he never went because my grandfather made him go to college. Robert only spent a short amount of time at school before he came home and started working for the family business. When I had questions about hockey, even when I was in the NHL, I called him. He had a feel for the game.

It's difficult to explain to people in the United States just how big hockey was in a town like Stirling. It's a very Canadian image: the mother and father sitting on the top steps of an arena, watching their son play hockey, probably sipping on coffee. That's exactly what it was like for me. My mom loves hockey to this day. My dad would sit and talk to the other fathers. It wasn't like it is now, when you hear stories about parents fighting. When I played in a tournament, the event was my parents' social time. I think the parents had more fun than we did playing in it. They'd sit around, have a few beers together, and talk. Nobody in our town had the money to travel and live lavish lives. Everybody was about the same.

There was no theater in town, so no one could see a movie in Stirling. Hockey was the main source of entertainment. People worked and went to the arena. I can still remember when we had a good juvenile team in town one year. Everyone in Stirling went to see the young guys play. The rink was packed, and it was good hockey too.

When I first started playing hockey, we were in one of those "dome" arenas. It would hold a few hundred. On some Saturday mornings I'd show up for a house league and there would be a sign on the door that said, "No hockey until the snow melts on the roof." It wasn't safe to be in there, so we had to wait until the afternoon when the sun came out and the snow melted. Then Stirling got a new arena that probably held 800 people or so. Remember, that's 800 in a town of maybe twice that. Everyone would be dressed in blue and yellow, because those were our hometown colors.

It's like that all across Canada. Towns have fund-raisers to pay for new buildings. And Stirling was great because it was small enough that there was always ice time for me. I didn't have to get up in the middle of the night to play hockey.

Of course, I didn't need a roof to want to play. We played on the pond at times, and we also had a cottage that was about ten minutes away and was right on a lake. In the winter, we'd clean the lake off and skate. If that weren't enough, we'd play ball hockey on the streets after dinner every night. I went through quite a few sticks that way. When I ran out, I'd go out to my dad and say, "I need a new stick." He'd look at me as if to say, "Again?" I'd crack a stick, and he'd get the Elmer's out and glue it together. He'd tape it up. Sometimes I had an inch of tape on my stick, just trying to hold it together. That's the way it was for us. Some of the kids today have matching uniforms. We were lucky to have a jersey of the same color for everybody. We had different helmets, socks, and pants. For Christmas, I'd always get a new pair of hockey socks and a stick, and I thought that was awesome.

I think I was lucky when it came to hockey at that point in my life. I had the opportunity to play a great deal, and with the help of my parents, I had the chance to develop my skills. Considering all the time I spent thinking about hockey growing up, you might think I had become obsessed with reaching the National Hockey League. I can't say that's correct. I did collect hockey cards and had magazines and pictures all over my room. The NHL was always a fantasy, though. I never really considered it as a possibility.

And it's not like there were a lot of role models for me at that time. When I was growing up, I had the chance to meet one NHL player: Nick Beverley. I never forgot it. I saw him at a hockey school in Halliburton. I've still got his autograph at home. And that was *Nick Beverley*. He was a good player, but not a superstar.

You could say I started climbing the ladder to the pros at age 13 or so. My big goal at that age was to play summer hockey because the good players did that. I got cut the first time I tried out for a summer team because I wasn't from a Triple-A center. I was from a D center, and they wouldn't let me play. That was about the worst thing that ever happened to me in hockey.

The next year, I tried out for a different summer league. It was in Pickering, almost all the way to Toronto. Two guys from Stirling and I tried out for the team and made it. We traveled to Toronto and Ottawa every weekend to play. Then in the summer of 1983, I got a tryout with the Trenton Bobcats of the Metro Junior B league. I made the team as a 15-year-old. That was a big change. The Junior B league had 20-year-olds playing in it. That's quite a jump from bantam hockey. I had to commute to practice in Trenton. It's about 20 miles, and Bruce Frye picked me up and took me to practice. Bruce's parents were customers of my dad's store.

When the team had road games, the closest trips were to Kingston and Peterborough, which were 45 minutes away. The other teams in the league were all around Toronto—Dixie, Markham, North York, and Newmarket. I'd leave late in the afternoon, play the game, and come back home late that night. And sometimes I still had school the next day. My parents always insisted that I go to school the next day no matter when I got home. They never let me miss school because of hockey.

I don't need to think about how often my mom had to drive me somewhere for a game. My dad always reminds me of that. He tells me how my mom wore out I don't know how many cars to take me to hockey. My reply is, "How much money did I save you by moving out of the house when I was 16?"

That first season with the Bobcats was the first for which I ever got paid. We earned $6 if we won, and got nothing if we lost or tied. When we'd win a game, the guys would all begin looking for the guy who paid us. "Where is he?" A man would hand out six bucks each, although I imagine the older guys got a little more. It was a big day when you got six dollars and a new stick. I didn't even get to pick out the sticks; they'd just hand me one. I didn't care. It was all pretty cool. When times were good, I got a new stick every ten days or so. And all that was awesome.

I didn't have a bad season for the Bobcats. I had 11 goals and ten assists in 40 games, and I only had 57 penalty minutes. Before I knew it, I was ready to try to take the next step, a Tier II team. I wasn't thinking of it as another step to the NHL. It was more a case of thinking that if I could do that, it would be unbelievable. I never, ever looked beyond the next step.

My parents allowed me to try out for a Tier II team, and another guy and I drove about 90 miles to try out for the team in Whitby. We thought it was pretty cool just to take one of my dad's company trucks for the weekend to drive up for the tryouts and then stay in a hotel overnight once we got there. Our hopes about actually making the team weren't too high. As it turned out, I made the team and my friend didn't.

I came home, and my parents said, "Now what?" I told them I would have to move into somebody's house next weekend, and I'd be going to school up there. Suddenly, decisions had to be made and arrangements had to be worked out.

Think about all of this: I was 16 years old, and I had to move away from home in order to play hockey. I didn't really make the decision. If my parents had said they wouldn't let me go, that would have been the end of my hockey career. I never would have known how far I could have gone. It would have been hard in the beginning, and I would have been back playing Junior B like I was before. My career would have been over at 20.

It's difficult to leave home at that age. You sacrifice a lot. I didn't really have friends for almost a year. I said good-bye to them from September to May, when I moved back home and finished school after the season was over. The only real friends I had were the guys on the team, and the only time I saw them was when I was at practice. But I had to play in that caliber of hockey if I wanted to be noticed.

The team made living arrangements with local families for its players. It paid for my room and board. Guys would be dropped off and be more or less told, "See ya. Here's your new home." On my first day away from home, I thought it was great at first, but later that day I looked around and said, "I'm stuck here." I was actually in Pickering, and everyone else on the team was in Whitby. I lived with a single mother who worked for the guy who owned the team. She had a child that was about two years old. They were never home. I had to learn how to cook my own dinners. I didn't have a car. I was hitching rides where I could. I still had to do schoolwork while playing hockey and trying to learn how to live on my own.

It was hell. I hated it.

I stayed with the woman and her child for about four months. Two of my teammates moved in with me for a while, and they eventually quit the team and moved out. I finally told the team I couldn't stay there any longer. "There's got to be something better," I said.

I moved in with a different family in Whitby, and it was great. They weren't rich, but they had meals, clean clothes, and a family atmosphere. I lived there with another guy on the team, John Hasty, and we split a basement room. The family had a husband and wife with two boys and a girl. At least when I switched schools, I knew somebody there. That kind of saved me. I met their friends, and I had a life again.

My new family just loved hockey, and they wanted to help out the team by putting a couple of us up. They went to all of our games, although sometimes watching us was a chore. We played more than

60 games that season, and we won nine of them. It was the only year Whitby had a team in that league. It was awful. I only played in 35 games. I had five goals and ten assists with 318 penalty minutes.

By the end of that season, I was thinking about the next step, which was the Ontario Hockey League. If you don't know about the system up there, the junior hockey teams have a draft that's a lot like the NHL draft. It was held in the North York Arena. It would be like American college football teams holding a draft of the best high school graduates and telling them where they had to go to school to play.

I didn't know if I was going to get drafted, but a few people told me to go just to experience it. A few other people in the area also had a chance of being drafted, so we all went. I remember sitting in the stands, watching guys get their names called as they were drafted and saying, "Wow, this is cool."

In the fifth round, I was sitting there and heard my name. I just went, "What?" Then everyone around me started saying, "Your name was just called!" My mom was all excited and didn't know what to do. I went down to meet everyone from the Cornwall Royals. They told me they had gone to see me a million times, but most of the times they came I was either kicked out or hurt or something. They didn't think they'd be able to get me. I went back to Stirling that night, and everyone I knew came over to my house. It was an exciting time. I knew at least I'd get a chance to try out for the OHL.

Cornwall is about two and a half hours east of Stirling. The Royals used to be in the Quebec junior league, and the team moved into the Ontario league. The Cornwall coach was Floyd Crawford, the father of Louie and Marc, and they were from Belleville. The head of player personnel was Gord Woods from Kingston. I figured I would just go to training camp, be cut, and get on with my life. A month before training camp, Floyd Crawford and Woods showed up at my house and I signed an OHL contract. They told us, "He's going to play this year. Sign the contract, and he'll join the team."

"You mean I don't even have to try out?" I asked.

"Just play the way you normally do, and you'll be on our team."

That was the first contract I ever signed. I think I got $21 a week in spending money along with room and board. I wasn't in much of a bargaining position, and I didn't care. They were at the house for hours, getting to know my family. We all asked a million questions about the whole experience. Before Gord passed away, he would always stop and talk to my parents for a couple of hours when he was passing through. He built a good relationship with them. It was nice.

I moved to Cornwall that fall and moved in with a family there along with the team's captain, Mike Bukowski. I thought I was pretty lucky. After the season started, I realized Mike was the biggest slob in the world. He was 19 or 20 at the time.

To top it all off, I wasn't exactly well fed. Out of seven days of the week, I bet we had pork chops, mashed potatoes, and frozen corn for four or five of those days. After a while, I'd look down at the pork chops and ask, "What is this?" It became an ongoing joke with the other guys on the team. They would talk about what they had for dinner. "We had steak. We had this. We had that," they said. Their families totally catered to them. I always had pork chops.

I said to myself, "I'm living with Bukowski and eating this?"

Pork chops make me roll my eyes to this day. And they weren't even good pork chops. I guess it was a learning experience, and I put up with it.

When I wasn't eating pork chops, I was pretty excited about playing major junior hockey. The OHL was the NHL to me. It was the real thing. I went through training camp, and there were older guys there along with guys who had been drafted by NHL teams. I was in awe.

It's funny to look back at the roster and remember the players behind the names. Ray Sheppard was at that first camp, and he was phenomenal. He scored 81 goals that year. It seemed like every time he touched the puck, it went into the net. Ray won the OHL scoring title with 142 points and was named the outstanding player in the league. Craig Duncanson was a first-round pick by Los Angeles. Mike Stapleton, who is Pat's son, was there too. Ken Sabourin was with the Capitals for a while; Steve Herniman had a long career in the minors; and Dan Nowak played with the German national team last I knew. Kent Trolley was from Belleville; I still keep in touch with him. Paul Cain eventually became my best friend on that team.

In my first OHL game, we got into a brawl with Oshawa. That was my welcome to the league. It was a full-fledged brawl. I was left thinking, "Is this what it's going to be like?" I think that was the biggest crowd I had ever played before—maybe three or four thousand people. That's more than the number of people in my hometown. I couldn't believe how many people were there when I was skating around in warm-ups. Everybody was into it, and it was great to be part of it.

I would have been pretty happy if that was as far as I went in hockey. A lot of guys never made it to that level. It was at a time when a lot of things were changing in my life. I was growing up—17 years old—and there was a lot going on. The hockey was good for me. It taught me discipline and respect. I was better at schoolwork. I might have overlooked those things for a few years, but I had to learn it quick. I guess I was a little different from the other kids my own age.

I didn't play much in my first year of junior, which made it tough. Coach Crawford was fired during the season, and Tony

Zappia replaced him. We used to call Zappia "Monty Hall," because it seemed like somebody was traded every day. We almost didn't want to go to the arena, because we were afraid we'd be next. We went through a ton of guys that season. It wasn't pleasant. I never knew what was going on.

At that age, I hadn't given any thought to trades until they started happening. There were big trades made in junior all the time. Some guys would move from city to city to city in less than a year. There was no stability whatsoever. And remember, these are kids who are 17, 18 years old who have to pack up and move. It must have been tough on those guys, but that's the way it was. I saw people lose interest in hockey and eventually quit after they got traded. They just wanted to get away from it.

I learned a lot in that first year. I had six goals and 13 assists with 253 penalty minutes in 1985-86, and our team was a little under .500. We were knocked out of the playoffs by Belleville in the first round.

Before the end of that season, I worked on a move that did wonders for me. I found out one of the other guys wouldn't be back for the next season. I knew he lived with a nice family, so I started laying the groundwork for the next year. "Mind if I move in next year? He'll be gone, and you'll have room," I said. They liked the idea, and that was the best thing that could have happened to me. I moved in with Bill and Lizette Robinson and their two daughters the following fall. One of their daughters was my age; the other was a few years younger. The parents always looked after everybody.

They saved me. No more pork chops.

The Robinsons' home was an unbelievable place to be. That was a second home for me. The year I left, my sister moved to Cornwall and became friends with them.

The team changed a great deal over the summer. Dale Hawerchuk and Scott Arniel, who at the time were NHL players and who later became my teammates with the Sabres, bought the team and owned it for the next couple of years. Whenever they came to Montreal, they dropped by.

"Monty Hall" was gone from the coaching job, and Orval Tessier replaced him. About a month after he took the job, Tessier called up Paul Cain, Steve Herninan, and me. "I want you guys to come to our house this afternoon," he said. "Rumor has it you guys are the main source of our off-ice problems."

I was like, "What? "What are you talking about?"

I guess Tessier had heard about our end-of-the-season party the year before. The night before we all packed up to go home, we went out to a place called the power dam, which is a dam operated by Ontario Hydro that runs from Cornwall across to Cornwall Island. We used to go out and camp there, have a few beers. My teammate John Copple had his truck all packed up to go home the next day, and he used to hunt when he went out there. So at some point in the night, he decided to pull out a shotgun out and fire two or three shots. We were all sitting around the campfire, and before we know it we hear, "Freeze! City Police!" We were speechless. Policemen came out of the woods and surrounded us. We were put in the cars and taken to town where we sat in jail overnight until someone from the team came and got us out.

So the three of us went out to Tessier's house, which was on the St. Lawrence River. We all got our good clothes on, a little afraid of what he'd say or do.

When he first saw us, he pointed down at the end of the road and said, "See that pile of railroad ties? Those big gooey railroad ties? I need them along my driveway," Tessier said. He gave us the keys to his truck and we drove down, loaded the railroad ties up, brought them up, and laid them down on the ground.

When we got done with that chore, Tessier said, "OK, come on down front." There he had a tarp over the water so that the weeds didn't grow through the surface. In the winter, Tessier would pull the tarp out and clean it off to put it away. Before we knew it, we were all scrubbing the tarp on our hands and knees.

After that, Tessier said, "All right, before you go home you can go inside and clean up, and before you go, my wife is going to feed you." She had a big spread on for us. We sat back and talked with him for the rest of the afternoon. He had tested us that day to see what sort of guys we were, and he was great to me from then on.

Under Tessier, my game improved a lot. I had 37 points in 46 games in 1986-87 (I broke my jaw along the way), and 52 points in 61 games in 1987-88. My penalty minutes went down from that first season and I became an assistant captain, so I was a leader of the team. That's when guys started looking at me differently. I got more respect and more responsibility.

Once I had been in the league a while and knew my way around, it was funny to see the "kids" come into the league. I recognized the look they had on their faces when they first arrived for junior hockey. I had had the same one. One of those players was Mathieu Schneider, who was a wide-eyed kid when he joined us in 1986. We heard a lot about him before he showed up, as he was going to be the next phenom. I gave him direction when he was 17. It was funny to see him in the NHL later. It's a good feeling to know I helped him along the way.

Looking at the scoring records of my junior teams is kind of like leafing through my high school yearbook. We had a few guys from those teams reach the NHL: Rick Tabaracci, Steve Maltais,

Stapleton, and Sheppard. I played against a ton of guys who made the pros. The best junior players I faced were people like Adam Graves, Andrew Cassels, and Brendan Shanahan.

Looking back, what strikes me is how many guys didn't make it, and alcohol was the big reason why. It was a big problem back then. There might have been a hundred guys who should have played pro hockey and didn't or who didn't fulfill their potential. The lifestyle contributed to alcohol abuse, and we didn't receive a great deal of supervision. We were all young kids, out on our own. Some teams monitored their players, but many others didn't. They were more worried about winning and losing. Some didn't even keep track of whether we were attending school. In our case, Tessier's brother was the principal of our high school, so the Royals kept track of us that way.

Things are better now. Between college and the pros, there are even more opportunities for young players to go on with hockey. Besides, the teams do a better job of looking after their players. That applies to the NHL teams, who bring in their draft choices for a few weeks over the summer to check up on them.

Junior hockey was rough but very good—fast, aggressive. Many of the best players were older than I was, and they were physically developed. At least I won a playoff series that final year. The season before, in 1986-87, we were knocked out by Ottawa in five games, so I was 0 for 2. Finally, in 1987-88, we had our best record in my three years, going 35-24-7, and we beat Belleville in six games in the first round. But that was it—we lost in five games to Ottawa. Final total: seven playoff wins in three years. Some might say that was pretty good practice for the early years in Buffalo.

By the time my third year was winding down, I was starting to think about the next step, the pros. It didn't take long for someone on the team to notice when scouts from NHL teams were at our games. They all sat in the same part of the rink. Someone from Central Scouting was there a lot as well. You'd hear, "Gotta go, gotta go, gotta show what I've got" a lot. I had been rated as a third-round prospect in the NHL draft in 1986 after my first season. Teams could draft 18-year-olds but only in the first three rounds. I wasn't taken. Two years later, I heard some rumblings that some teams might be interested in me. I got some questionnaires from teams such as Hartford and Washington. It was exciting to know someone was paying attention.

Everyone in junior hockey was in awe of anyone who had a connection to the pros. When a teammate was going to a pro training camp in the fall, there would be a line to take him to the airport or pick him up. When our season was over, some of the drafted players would be called up to play in the minors. We thought those guys were awesome.

At that point, though, I didn't know what was ahead of me. I figured I'd be heading back to Stirling. I was very wrong about that.

4

DRAFTED

A car pulled into my driveway in Stirling on June 10, 1988. I was getting a ride to Montreal for the next day's NHL draft.

I didn't know if I was going to be drafted or not; it was exciting just to go to the draft to see what it was like. I didn't have a great many expectations. It's not like I was going to be taken in the first round. I was just hoping to go in the later rounds or maybe get invited to a pro training camp. My family didn't even bother to make the drive. I guess we all felt that it was better for everyone to stay home in case I wasn't drafted. My friends were pretty excited about the whole process. They wondered what was going to happen. The NHL draft was so foreign to everyone in my area; no one from Stirling had ever been picked.

I got into the car and said hello to my agent, Rollie Thompson. Then I realized that sitting next to me was—of all people—Tie Domi from Toronto. He played for Peterborough and was two years behind me but had a chance to go in the early rounds. We had run into each other a few times in junior hockey.

I "whacked out" when I saw him in the car. It was so unexpected; I was just so startled to see him. It was a very quiet trip to Montreal.

I talked to Rollie a little but had no conversation with Tie.

Once we got to Montreal, Tie and I found we were sharing a hotel room, and it didn't take very long for us to get into a fight in it. I don't remember that the fight was about anything in particular. Eventually, he hit his head on the corner of the nightstand, and that was the end of it. The two of us got along fine the rest of the time. In fact, it was a fun weekend.

There was so much going on. All of the players hung around the hotel that night. Agents, players, and coaches were there too. The top prospects were going around for interviews and meetings with different teams, but I only had one meeting. The Sabres had me in for an interview.

Gerry Meehan was the general manager then, and Ted Sator was the coach. Don Luce, the director of player personnel, was there, as were a couple of scouts. I was scared to death walking into the hotel room for the interview. They asked me all about my career, what my best assets were, how I could help a team, future plans outside of hockey, and so on. It took about a half hour. Gerry was impressive but not intimidating. I got pretty comfortable while I talked to him. Ted was the same way. I walked away feeling pretty good about the interview, but it's not like I was convinced the Sabres would take me. I didn't know anything about the process. I was so green then it was pitiful. I was just happy I could say, "Yeah, I talked to Buffalo." It was cool they were interested.

Rollie had someone at the draft to look after us, and about four or five of us went out for dinner. It turned into a fairly late night, but it felt good just to keep my mind occupied. Some of the other guys raised a little hell. The drinking age in Quebec was only 18, so they had a lot of fun.

I sort of slept that night, and the next morning we were rounded up and taken over to the Forum for the draft. I can still picture the scene—I was on the same side as the door to the Canadiens' dressing room, halfway up on the lower section. The first round took forever. The guys had to go on stage and pose for pictures and all that. Even though I figured I'd have a wait, there still was some anxiety before each pick in the first round. Some general manager would get ready to announce their pick, and I'd say to myself, "Is it going to be me? Is it going to be me?" Then some guy's name would be read, and I'd exhale. It would be a letdown. Then it would be the next team's turn, and I'd go through the same feelings again.

Mike Modano was the first player taken that year, followed by Trevor Linden. The Ontario Hockey League didn't have that many stars taken that year. Darrin Shannon went fourth. I played with him briefly and with his brother, Darryl, for quite a while in Buffalo. Domi went to Toronto in the second round.

Once the draft gets past the first round, the real wait begins. Every year, families come to the draft and sit and wait until their loved one's name gets called, and then there's a burst of applause and hugging in one corner of the arena. You don't realize how long that wait is until you've actually been through it. In hindsight, it probably wasn't that long. The draft was a little quicker back then, since they did it all in a day, but it was awful at the time. One of the worst parts was when someone I knew was taken ahead of me. "What? Are you kidding me? This is crap," I thought to myself.

As the draft went along, I was left to sit by myself. My agent ran around talking to people, and once in a while he gave me an update on my situation. "Such-and-such a team is talking about you," he'd say, and then he'd go away. I'd look down on the floor of the Forum and see the guys who had been chosen, walking around with their jerseys on. I really felt like going down and smacking somebody.

Finally, my name was called in the fifth round—97th overall—by Buffalo. I don't think my whole name was out of Gerry Meehan's mouth before I was at the bottom of the stairs. A public relations guy shook my hand and guided me over to the Sabres table. I met about a dozen guys there. One of them said, "We weren't sure if you'd still be around in the fifth round. Everyone is so happy that you were still there." I was in such a fog at that point, I just mumbled, "Really? Um, why didn't anyone come tell me that?"

I called my parents right from the draft table to tell them I had been picked. It was such a thrill to put on an NHL jersey and pose for a picture in front of the NHL logo. The Sabres gave me a box of stuff. It had a T-shirt, some pins, and other collectibles, and I thought that was just awesome. I couldn't wait to take it home to show everyone. "Look at the box of stuff they gave me," I said. Once the pictures were taken, someone came over and asked for the jersey back. They needed it for the next draft choice. "Do I have to?" I asked.

I was the Sabres' pick after Alexander Mogilny. As it turned out, we stayed in the league a lot longer than their top picks. Joel Savage went to Buffalo in the first round and Darcy Loewen went in the third. The Sabres also took Keith Carney in that draft, so they were pretty good at picking in the late rounds.

After the draft, the Sabres had a little reception for all of their draft picks. Joel, Darcy, and I were there, and we got to spend some time together and talk to everyone who was there with the Sabres.

When I got home in the early afternoon the next day, it seemed like half of the town was waiting for me. That was nice, but once they left it was fun to sit and tell my family about the whole weekend. The experience was great for me, but I think it was even better for the members of my family. I was a Sabre.

If I had any thoughts about getting a big head about being drafted, they ended quickly. After getting home on Sunday, I went to work at the shop on Monday. "It's seven o'clock. Time to get out of bed. Let's go," my dad yelled. He didn't really care I had become an NHL player.

I can't say I prepared too much for my first pro training camp. A month before, I started skating and running. I thought I was in decent shape, but I really wasn't. I didn't know what to expect. The Sabres sent me material in the mail every so often—visa information, housing, and so forth, but there wasn't a word about a contract.

I figured that a pro training camp might be the climax of my career. I just wanted to see what it was like. I didn't let myself think about starting a long pro career. Let me put it this way: when I left home for camp, I had enough clothes in a bag for a week or so, and that was it. I wasn't thinking about staying any longer than that.

My dad gave me $20 in American currency when I was getting ready to leave. "You're going to need some American money when you get down there," he said. I jumped in my car and drove to suburban Buffalo in September. The actual camp was in Wheatfield, near Niagara Falls.

The Sabres gave me a few hundred dollars for meal money right at the start of camp, and that looked pretty good. I said something like, "Look at this—let's eat." And it was off to McDonald's.

I remember sitting in the dressing room, just staring across at the captain, Lindy Ruff. Mike Ramsey, Mike Foligno, and those guys were all there. Under my breath I said, "Look at those guys!" I was just in awe of NHL players. My first memory of Tom Barrasso is pretty distinctive. On the first day of practice, someone shot high on him. Barrasso chased him down the ice, throwing his stick and generally having a tantrum. "What is this all about?" I said to myself. My eyes were opened in a big hurry.

The young guys on the team did the most talking. Players such as Jeff Parker and Benoit Hogue showed off a little in the locker room. I just sat there and didn't say a word. None of the Sabres really tried to make friends with the rookies. There were too many of us around. I hung around with a few rookies. We were all in the same boat, so we stuck together. You see players do that to this day.

After several years with the Sabres, I tried to talk to as many kids as I could to make them feel comfortable. For a while that wasn't the case. I tried the old intimidation tactic because I was insecure about my job. I figured if I went crazy in the first few days, no one would come near me. Eventually, though, I remembered what camp was like for a rookie, and I was secure enough not to worry about my job.

It was all a little scary at the time, though. I had never skated with guys who were that fast and that good. It took a little while just to catch up to that mentally. I was told by just about everyone to leave an impression during training camp—good, bad, or whatever, but make sure the coaches noticed you. That's the attitude I took into camp. I didn't get into a fight every day, but I tried to play hard.

Early in camp, every day that I wasn't assigned somewhere else or cut was a good day. The players were split into a bunch of teams for practices, and I listened to some of the guys who had been through a few camps before. They'd say they only had a certain amount of meal money left, so they could guess as to when cuts would be made. Sure enough, some guys were cut or sent back to junior hockey right on time, but I stuck around. I exhaled and practiced some more.

Once the intrasquad scrimmages were over, we were getting ready to start the exhibition season when I almost threw away any chance I had at playing pro hockey—or so I thought. The veterans told the rest of us, "We're all going down to the Locker Room," a bar in Buffalo. Scott Metcalfe, Kevin Kerr, and I went down there together. Scott and I became friends pretty quickly in camp.

After a while, we decided that we should get back to the hotel and get some sleep for the next day's practice. We left before most of the other guys. Scott and I were in the back seat of a Jeep, while Kevin and some girl were in the front seat. We were about a hundred yards down Delaware Avenue when Kevin started talking to the girl. He lost his concentration, and we veered off the side of the road and hit one of those big steel light poles near the fence that borders Forest Lawn Cemetery.

The Jeep had a soft top on it, and I hit my head on the roll bar. It knocked me out cold. Scott was fine, the girl was bounced around a little, and Kevin got burns on his arms and legs because he hit the pavement. Once I came to, I noticed my ears were blue and swollen. I couldn't even touch them.

We all thought, "We are done. We're out of here."

The next day, Gerry Meehan called us into his office, wanting to know what happened. We told the story, and he read us the proverbial riot act. Meehan fined us a few hundred dollars each, and sent us to the team doctor to be checked out. As I was walking out, I thought to myself, "How can he fine me? I don't get paid. Do I have to pay this on my own? How does this work?" I don't think I ever paid that fine, by the way.

Two days later we had an exhibition game in Norfolk, Virginia, against the Washington Capitals. I got to play, and I was a little wired up. Jim Pizzutelli and Rip Simonick, our trainer and equipment manager respectively, were on my side, and they had helped fire me up.

That was the first time I had ever worn a Sabres uniform. Believe me, I took a good look in the mirror to see how it looked. I went out on to the ice and saw the reflection in disbelief. Even at the end of my career, I used to catch myself checking out the sweater. That was a good sign—I was still excited about wearing an NHL jersey and didn't take anything for granted.

The game started, and on my first shift I made it from the bench to the center ice dot. I immediately got into a fight with Jim Thomson, who was the Capitals' tough guy. I did great in the fight, and was thrown out for starting it. I must have played five seconds. When I came off the ice, I felt pretty good about how the fight went, even though my ears were bleeding. That was my only exhibition game for the Sabres that season.

A couple of days later, I was assigned to Rochester. The Sabres never said I'd play down there; I was just assigned to the Americans. I didn't really think of it as being "cut." I thought it was just another opportunity. I still didn't have a contract, and I was still scared to death about what might happen.

We practiced down in Rochester for a couple of weeks, and before I knew it, opening night had arrived. I still hadn't signed a contract at that time, but the team had indicated that I'd be playing that night. I called my agent a lot to try to find out what was going on, and we agreed just to see what happened.

About 20 minutes before the start of warm-ups, Joe Crozier of the Sabres' organization came into the locker room. He growled, "Sign this."

"Sign what?" I replied.

"Sign this in case you get hurt tonight. You're playing."

"Really? What is this?"

"It's a contract. Just sign it. We'll worry about it later."

It could have been for a million dollars or ten dollars, and I wouldn't have known the difference. I didn't care. I had made the team.

"Where do I sign?"

That was the extent of my first contract negotiations. I didn't know how much I'd get. I signed anyway. We played Hershey that night, and to this day I don't remember a single detail about that game. The next day, I looked at the contract a little closer. I received a $13,000 signing bonus and a $25,000 AHL contract for the season. It went up to $27,500 the next year and $30,000 the year after that. Everyone got paid the same, more or less. I called home, and my father's first reaction was, "Is that $25,000 American?"

We got paid every two weeks, and the signing bonus was in the first check. I felt like I had won the lottery or something. I had to go open a checking account that day. I didn't buy a car or anything like that. A lot of guys sign their first pro contracts and spend their bonus in about a week, but I put my money in the bank. Still, life was good.

That first season in Rochester, 1988-89, was probably the best year of my life. It was the first time I had lived away from home on my own. I stayed in a hotel for a while, and then I moved in with Scott Metcalfe and Kevin Kerr in a dumpy old house. We didn't spend a whole lot of time in it. It seemed like we were out every night. There were girls and parties and so forth. I look back now and wonder how I survived the year. There was a lot of excitement in that house. I don't know if we ever took out the garbage; we sort of piled it up in the garage. Kevin was kind of a moody guy. He'd fall hard for girls, and Scott and I would give him a hard time about it. We had some fights over that sort of thing, but otherwise we had way too much fun. I guess it was a good learning experience. At least I didn't do anything too stupid.

The minors are a good place to learn about the game. I would say there's twice as much coaching as there is in the NHL. I think by the time you get to the NHL, you know what your role is. Coaching in the NHL is about coming up with a breakout or a power play plan—game situations. Down there, it's more about honing skills. I think that's harder than teaching a system. You can show a diagram on the board and say, "This is the way we're going to forecheck," and guys are intelligent enough to go out and try to do it at least. That's what a coach does in the NHL—break down the other team. In the minors, they teach the skills so that you can go do it on the ice.

John Van Boxmeer was a pretty demanding coach. He would call people out in front of the team and criticize them. I think he learned a little from Scotty Bowman; he played for Scotty in Montreal and Buffalo. Boxy would embarrass players. But I think Boxy was good for the young guys. He made us go that extra mile. He got in your head and twisted it around a bit and got the best out of you.

One time early in the season, Boxy came to me and said, "The only way you're going to make the NHL is to take (Kevin) Maguire and (Mike) Hartman's job."

"So what's that mean?" I said.

"You're going to have to play that role."

I had never really fought in junior. I got in a few fights a year, but I was never a huge fighter. When he said that, I went, "Whoa—is there anything else I can do instead of this?" I went on to get 446 penalty minutes that year. Down there, they want to win, but the coach's job was to produce players who could help in Buffalo. The older players taught the younger players. They didn't mind if I took a bad penalty as long as I improved. I had my butt handed to me so many times down there, but it was the only way to learn. I kept doing it and doing it and doing it. I don't know how I ever made it through that season.

Sometimes I looked at it all and said, "What am I doing? I'm a hockey player." I'd go games without touching the puck. I'd play for a minute and a half and then get thrown out. "Is this really what I want to do?" But the more I did it, the more comfortable I became with it, and the more I understood that it was what I needed to do in order to play. I wanted to play so badly that I did whatever it took.

It didn't take long to develop a name and a reputation around Rochester. Scott and Kevin had been there the previous year, and they were popular for their physical play. Van Boxmeer put the three of us together to form a line. Among the three of us, we ended up with 993 penalty minutes. Every time we went out on the ice, fans became jacked up because they knew something was going to happen. Other teams went running when we came on the ice.

In Cape Breton one night, we got into a brawl involving our whole line. Scott had a guy bent along the boards, and I remember him saying, "Hit him, Rayzor. Hit him." I kept hitting him. We went from guy to guy like that. If somebody did that now, he'd be suspended for the entire season. He'd never play.

Scott and Kevin knew everyone in town, so it made it easy for me to meet people. I was recognized all over Rochester, constantly signing autographs. This was all new for me, and at the time I thought it was pretty neat.

When I managed to find time to get to the ice, I discovered it was good hockey—rough, but good. For the first couple of months, I never got on the ice for long. I don't know if Van Boxmeer was trying to make me angry or hungry or what. Eventually, he gave me a chance, and I didn't want to give him the opportunity to sit me again. I tried to hone my game in order to get ready for a shot at the NHL.

I liked Van Boxmeer as a coach. He was a tough guy and a tough coach, but he got the best out of me. Boxy is the type of guy who likes to be in control of situations. He'd be good in the NHL, but I think he's happier as a general manager and coach in the minors. That way no one tells him what to do.

Boxy had a good relationship with his players. I remember one time Boxy came into the dressing room and was screaming at all of us. Then Richie Dunn, a veteran who was finishing up his career in Rochester, told Boxy to "shut the [heck] up."

I was sitting there thinking, "What? What did he say to the coach?"

It was all part of the learning experience. I wasn't playing with kids anymore. These were grown men with families playing for their livelihood—the typical mixture of veterans and prospects. The best players—Ken Priestlay, Mike Donnelly, Bob Halkidis, Mikael Andersson—would go up to Buffalo quite a bit when someone was hurt, and then when the injured guy would heal, they'd came back. A lot of the guys who went up to the NHL were bitter when they came back. Really bitter. "Why should I have to come back while such-and-such is still up?" they'd say. I think everyone in that position feels that way for a while. In addition, players would be jealous when someone else got called up to the Sabres. "Why him? Why not me?" they'd ask. I didn't experience that my first year. I was just happy to be in the pros.

Jody Gage was one of our top scorers. He had been around the AHL for quite a while and had a contract worth $60,000, which made him about the highest-paid player in the league. That was huge to someone like me.

Keith Gretzky was on that team too. He was always a guy who liked to be the center of attention when we were in the dressing room. Keith wanted to be the one chasing women. He never took the game too seriously. He was a good player, but he was more interested in everything but hockey. I think one of his problems was having the expectations that come with being Wayne Gretzky's brother. I played against Keith in junior, and he was pretty good. When he got to the pros and realized that he wasn't going to make it big, he took the attitude that he was just going to have fun.

Those expectations are tough. Look at Wayne Primeau, who was a first-round draft choice of the Sabres. Everyone looked at him and thought he was going to be just like his brother, Keith. But he's not the same player. As soon as everyone realizes things like that, we'll all be better off.

Wayne Van Dorp also played for us. Wayne had quite a reputation. He lived in a 1956 Fargo van—flat front, square and boxy look—when he first got to Rochester. He finally got a place to live when it got cold out. One time Wayne and the rest of us went to Steve Smith's for dinner. We had some sort of pie for dessert, and someone put shaving cream instead of whipped cream on top the piece served to Wayne. Van Dorp took a big mouthful of it and then spit it out. He got so mad I thought he was going to cry right there. He walked out of the place and never came back. Wayne was bitter for the rest of his time in Rochester.

We went through five goalies that season. Darcy Wakaluk played more than any of them. You couldn't talk to him before the game. He tried to stay in a zone, completely focused before and during the game.

Goalies handle the pressure differently. If you tell some guys that they are going to play the next day, they'll be a basket case right up until game time. Dominik Hasek is usually in a "zone," so you stay away from him before and during the game. Marty Biron never shuts up. He yaps during every stoppage of play. He'll say, "Nice pass out there" or something like that.

I didn't have the right to do much yapping at the start of my career. The last game before Christmas that year, I scored my second point of the season. I guess I caught on to my role after that, because I had 29 points by the end of the season. I earned some playing time, and I got plenty of room to operate out on the ice.

My family back home followed my career as best they could. It sounds kind of primitive now, but they used to drive up to the top of a hill near Stirling and listen to the games on radio. The signal could come in right over Lake Ontario, and that was the best place to hear the Rochester station. It became easier when I got them a dish to watch my games. I used to call my parents collect all the time back then. In fact, I called that way until about 1995, and they always accepted the charges. They were always interested in what I was doing. After a few years, we talked about everything but hockey.

By the end of the season, I felt pretty good. The team missed the playoffs even though it had a winning record, but I won rookie of the year and most improved player. I still didn't have any aspirations about playing for the Sabres, but I felt like I could play in the pros for a while longer. Driving home for the summer, I felt like I had accomplished something.

I had only a couple of weeks to enjoy the break, and then it was right back to the store for the summer, which went by quickly. Before I knew it, I was back at training camp in the fall of 1989. That camp was a lot more comfortable. I knew a lot of the guys already and felt almost relaxed going in because I knew what to expect.

Rick Dudley was the new coach of the Sabres at that camp. Duds was a little more hands-on than Ted Sator. He was a fitness freak. I think that was when I first realized that the team expected players to be in shape right from the start. Everyone was sore at the start of camp, and everyone complained about it. Nobody had ever had to work so hard before.

I was still in awe of some of the big names, like Rick Vaive. But I looked around to see how the guys who played my role were doing. Everyone else didn't really matter. Exhibition games were a chance to impress some people. I tried to do that, but I can't say I was surprised when I was assigned to Rochester with a bunch of other guys after a few weeks of camp.

I figured I'd be spending another full season in the minors. I was wrong.

5

A MEMORABLE DEBUT

Every player remembers his first NHL game. I just didn't know at the time that mine was going to be a statistical highlight of my career.

I had played the night before—October 20, 1989—in Rochester. I had no idea the call was coming. I came in off the ice and was told to go and see John Van Boxmeer, the coach. I went in, and he said, "You're going up." I said, "Yeah, right." I kind of giggled.

"No, seriously," Boxy said. "You've got to be at the airport to fly to Pittsburgh tomorrow. You'll meet the team, practice with them, and play."

The possibility of playing in the NHL really hadn't come up in my head before that. In training camp in 1989, I got to play a couple of games with the Sabres in preseason, but I still never thought about going up. I had started the season in Rochester. When I got the call, it was totally unexpected.

I was pretty excited, but when I told some of the guys in the dressing room, they were a little ticked off because I was the one going and they weren't. They looked at me in a funny way, and it gave me a difficult feeling. I tried to get out of the arena as quickly as possible.

It might seem like it's the wrong attitude to say, "Why him?" But it's like that for aspiring players. If you don't have that attitude in part, you're in the wrong business. You always think you should be the one who should be going up. If you lose that, you're done playing.

I went home and called everyone I knew. "I'm going up, I'm going up." I didn't know if I was going to play or not, but I didn't care. By the way, nobody sleeps in that situation, and I didn't either.

I flew into Pittsburgh the next morning in time for the morning skate. Once I got there, everything was new. When I left the Civic Arena, I wondered, "Where do I go for lunch?" I didn't know there was a team meal. When I looked around that day and saw guys like Rick Vaive and Mike Foligno—guys whom I watched growing up—I shook my head and said, "Here I am. What am I going to do?"

The coaches had told me that morning that I'd be playing and that my linemates would be Scott Arniel and Kevin Maguire. I thought, "Great. Who cares?" Rick Dudley, the head coach, had a brief conversation with me. He said just to go out and play the game that I had been playing in Rochester. "I don't know how much I'll be able to get you in or when I'll be able to get you in, but just be ready to go," he said. The guys were telling me to relax because they didn't know what to expect out of me either. They hadn't really seen me other than in training camp, and I didn't really know anybody. Ray Sheppard was the only guy I really knew, because I had played junior with him. There wasn't much of a comfort zone.

I didn't sleep during the day either. My roommate was Doug Bodger, and I asked him a million questions. "What do you do? Where do we go? What do we have to do? What's next?" I didn't know. Doug looked at me and said, "Shut up, let me sleep."

I was 21 years old. I didn't know what to expect. Everything was trial and error. I had to sit back and be cautious. I was afraid to say anything to anyone.

After one of the longest afternoons of my life, I walked over to the Civic Arena. Guys are always there early, doing their thing to get ready for the game. In the minors, you don't have that opportunity. You arrive on a bus, get off the bus, throw your equipment out there, get dressed, and play. You're never there early. In the majors, your equipment is there the night before. Once everyone arrived, we had meetings before the game. Even that was different. We never had a meeting in the minors.

Finally, warm-up came along. I put the jersey on to get ready to play. I guess I knew I had made it up to the NHL before that, but it really hit me when I was actually dressed and going out on the ice. I thought to myself, "OK, am I ready for this?"

I was in a fog. I looked down at the other end of the ice and saw Mario Lemieux, Paul Coffey—all those guys on the Penguins. I was trying to get ready for the game, but I wanted to check everything out, too. Heck, I kept staring at the people in the stands. There were more people there than there had been for any of the games in Rochester. My eyes probably were as big as beach balls. I was trying to take in a million things all at once. It was kind of an overload.

I think I ran into Dean Kennedy in warm-up—ran right into him and wiped out. That woke me up. "OK, get your head going here. Straighten it out." I realized I had to clear my mind and be ready.

The game finally started. My line sat there on the bench for about ten minutes. All of a sudden Dudley said we were going out. I looked back and said, "Are you sure?" He said, "Yeah, go." So we went.

We broke out of our end on the first shift. At the time I was playing left wing, and I went down the left wing wall. Mike Ramsey carried it out of the zone, came across the blue line toward the red line and hit me between the red line and the far blue line. As soon as I went over the blue line, I looked up and the defense was backing off. I shot from just about the top of the circle. I never saw the puck again.

There was a major delayed reaction. Suddenly the guys came over with their arms up in the air, and I was like, "What happened?" I still didn't know. I was in a blackout. Finally I realized the puck was in the net. I thought, "Oh …" Tom Barrasso, who had been traded to the Penguins by the Sabres, was the goalie; it went five-hole on him. It was probably the farthest shot I ever took that went in.

Everyone was happy for me, cheering me on. I came back to the bench, sat down, and said, "This is nothing. Where have I been? Why didn't I get this opportunity earlier? This isn't as hard as I thought it would be."

The whole game, it seemed like everything went right. We played well and won, 4–2. I wound up with a goal and an assist, and was a +3. Statistically, that was the best game I ever had in the NHL. I've still got the game sheet. When I went down to the minors after 27 games, I had two goals and an assist and was a –5.

That night I even had Rob Brown of the Penguins calling me out, wanting to fight me. Little Rob Brown. I came up to Buffalo to be a physical player, but I was like, "I'm on a roll here. I've got two points. I'm not wasting my time in the penalty box."

After the game, the guys were pretty happy for me. They knew what sort of player I was supposed to be, so it was funny to see me score. Duds looked at me as if to say, "Don't forget why we brought you up here." Guys like Maguire and Mike Hartman were thinking they should become "players" instead of doing what they were supposed to do—play physical—and that's what he wanted out of me.

***

That team had an interesting mix of talent. Pierre Turgeon was the top scorer. He had been drafted number one overall in 1987. Everybody looked at him as "the guy." I was about the same age as he was. Sometimes I just looked at the things he did and went, "Wow."

It's funny—when I was drafted, I couldn't have named you three guys on the Buffalo Sabres. Once I joined the organization, I started paying attention, and Pierre was the guy everyone was talking about. He was young and he had a lot of pressure on him to play well. He concentrated more on his play than on things like leadership. He wasn't a guy who stood up in the dressing room, but because Pierre was the number-one overall pick, the team was desperate for him to lead it to the promised land. I think that was a big part of the problem with him in Buffalo. The Sabres put way too much pressure on him, and he didn't have the personality to handle that. He was a young kid just trying to prove himself.

Pierre was a pretty good symbol for that team. It didn't have those one or two people who would tell the team, "This is how we do it." There were some guys who were skilled but went in all different directions. It was not a "team" team.

I had watched Rick Vaive play for the Maple Leafs when I was growing up. He was a 50-goal scorer. Rick was "Squid" or "The million-dollar man." When I came to Buffalo, he was making $400,000. That was by far more than anyone else in the dressing room. We looked at that number and said, "Man, that is unbelievable." On the side of his Cooper helmet, he had little stickers with dollar signs on them.

Rick was a super guy. He's a different person now than he was then. He was sort of a wild man who lived life to the fullest and had a lot of fun. Now he doesn't even drink. Rick wore more equipment than any player I've ever seen. People used to call him "Robocop" because every part of his body was covered. When he stood in front of the net, he took a beating but didn't think anything about it. I looked at him like the way I looked at Dave Andreychuk—two guys who couldn't be moved from in front of the net. That's where they got a lot of their goals. Squid didn't score by blasting in from coming down the wing. He got it out front by jamming away.

When Andreychuk was here, he and John Tucker were the young guys on the team who were out having a good time. Everyone looked to them for the story about what happened the night before. They were the life of the team. They joked around in the room, and always knew where to go and what to do. Everybody looked at them and said, "What's going on?" They treated everyone well.

When Dave came back to Buffalo in 2000, after more than seven years, it was funny to remember that he had played more than 700 games as a Sabre. Some of the fans around here looked at him with a shrug and said, "Oh, it's just Dave Andreychuk." Are you kidding me? At the time, people thought I had been a Sabre forever, and Dave had played 50 more Sabres games at that point than I had, and he had been gone for seven years.

You can't ask for a better guy around the room. You can't ask for a guy who would do more for you. He worked his butt off. I think back to when he was here the first time, he was young and maybe he didn't work as hard as he did later in his career. I know that every game we played against him after he left, we talked about him before the game. "Watch this guy," we said. "Great hand-eye coordination. One of the best I've ever seen with a puck and a stick."

Dave sort of relied on talent early in his career, but he came to realized it takes more than that. And even though he was always a guy who scored 30 or more goals every year, people got on him for not scoring in the playoffs. Well, for years, what Sabre did? Nobody. That was our problem. It's pretty hard to point the finger at one guy and say, "He was the reason why."

Phil Housley was on that '89 team. He is one of the few guys in hockey that I dislike. Phil was a guy who thought he was far above me and a lot of other people. He had an attitude; he looked at people like they weren't supposed to be there.

Housley was a phenomenal talent, but when he was interviewed, it was "me, me, me, me, me. I'm the best. I'm this. I'm that." The first thing he started talking about when others were around was what he had, what he'd done, and how he was playing.

It was the same with Christian Ruuttu, who was also on that team. He came up to me one time and said, "You should just thank me for being here."

"Why would I thank you for you being here?" I asked.

"If it wasn't for me, you probably wouldn't be here."

Thanks a lot.

It doesn't take very long to pick up on what people are like when you join a team. You sort of sit back and look. Sometimes guys talk about themselves for different reasons, but when it happens every day, you know what these guys are like. Phil liked Alexander Mogilny because Alex was the new thing coming in. With me, Phil's attitude was "Pfft, sorry."

Mogilny was a carefree guy who did his own thing—happy-go-lucky, but very, very, very private. He never opened up to a lot of people; he had his own friends on the side. Alex acted like he didn't understand much English, but I think he knew more than what he let on. That was a good excuse for a while. Dominik Hasek was the same way when he came here.

When Alex finally got to America after defecting from the Soviet Union, he expected a lot more than Buffalo had to offer. His ideas about the United States came from the TV and from what he imagined New York and Los Angeles to be like. Then he rolled into Buffalo, and he must have thought, "What is this? This kind of reminds me of home." That was his biggest problem—he had some culture shock in thinking that the Buffalo would be more different from home than it was.

During that first season he went through a period where he wasn't flying and had a lot of problems. I believe to this day that it might have been part of a ploy to get traded or something. But personally, he was a good guy. If he liked you, he liked you. It just took a lot for him to trust people and get to know them. I think a couple of guys took him under their wings, and he became comfortable with them, but he wasn't a guy who would call you up and say, "Let's go out for a beer." He had his friends in the game and his friends out of the game, and that was it.

Guys such as Turgeon and Mogilny were about my age and had such breathtaking talent. I looked at them and said, "I'm on the same team as these guys, and I'm not that good. I'm not nearly as good as they are. How the hell am I here?"

Throughout my career, I had to remind myself that I was considered one of the top 650 players in the world. It was kind of hard to fathom at times, because some days nothing went right and I would say, "There's got to be someone better than me out there to do this job. If I'm like this, how bad are the other guys?" Mogilny would go by me at a hundred miles per hour, and I'd just say, "Wow."

Mike Ramsey was a top defenseman on the team. Rammer is Rammer, and he's the same to this day. He worked his butt off every night. He'd cut his arm off to win a game. Sometimes he couldn't separate everyday life from the game. He was one of those guys whose life was the game.

Uwe Krupp, another defensemen, was a guy I always thought could be a better player than he was. One time at Sabreland, our practice facility, I said he was chicken, and he backed me up against the wall in a corner and said, "Don't you ever call me that." I said, "Play different on the ice, and I won't have to." He and I never saw eye to eye.

Our goaltenders were Daren Puppa and Clint Malarchuk. Daren was the starting goalie most of the time. That year, he was phenomenal. We had a real hot streak early in the season when I was there, and he was a big part of it.

Clint was a Jekyll and Hyde. He had trouble with his wife, and had a great deal going on his life. Day to day, I never knew what kind of guy he was going to be, but he was funny. He is one of the funniest guys I've ever played with. Clint was always pulling jokes, entertaining the guys. He always had something going on. Clint was a laid-back cowboy who seemed to say, "Give me a bar stool and some cowgirls to look at, and I'm happy." He kept things alive and exciting.

When Clint finally left, it was nasty. He was having depression problems at the time. Here's an example: there's a scene in the movie *Slap Shot* where the coach says, "It must be true, Dickie Dunn wrote it." So one time Clint said something, and I said, "Ah, it's got to be true. Dickie Dunn wrote it." I was just joking around, and Clint flipped out on me. He got me in the clothes room and said, "Don't you ever say that about him. He's a friend of mine." It scared the crap out of me. He would go off like that sometimes. You never knew what you'd get out of him.

That was a cliquey team. There were some huge changes going

on in the dressing room. That was the time when the NHL Players' Association was having its problems with Alan Eagleson. I remember one day Kennedy and Maguire got in a fight in the dressing room—literally fought at Sabreland, our practice facility. Kennedy hated Eagleson, but Maguire loved him because Eagleson had helped him do stuff in Toronto. They thought two different ways, and they fought like crazy. The NHLPA meetings were like a war zone—the guys were so split. It was terrible. We were voting to get rid of Eagleson, and I didn't know much about it. I went to guys I trusted and said, "Who do I vote for? What do I do?" That was a really awful time. And the issue split a lot of other dressing rooms around the league as well, because everyone wasn't equal back then.

It was a funny feeling to be dropped into the middle of all of that after the start of the season. It's different from being on the team from the start of training camp. I didn't really have a chance to know the guys before I played. I lived in a hotel for a while when I first came up. I walked from the arena back to the hotel, and I was by myself. I had a world at the arena, but as soon as I walked away from it, I had no friends, no family, no nothing.

But back then, at least guys had fun. We were together a lot more than the players are now. There was more of a team unity—not so much on the ice, but off the ice. That made it easier. Guys would go to lunch every day and hang out together. We'd sit there at lunch until someone had to go home for dinner, and it would be the same thing the next day.

Now guys aren't relaxed. They don't have fun. Their lives are hockey. They are totally dedicated. They look after themselves so much that their minds don't have an opportunity to get away from it. They're too involved with everything that's going on instead of walking away from the arena and having a life away from it.

The reason for that, I think, is the money. Players are worried about the business side, but back then, everyone made about the same. Vaive made about $400,000, and I probably was at the bottom at $95,000, if that. That's about a $300,000 spread, and the remaining 20 guys fell within that range. By 2004, when I played my last game, some players earned $11 million and some earned "only" $400,000. That's a pretty big spread.

But that first NHL game check still looked good when I arrived shortly after that game in Pittsburgh. I think in the minors I made $27,500, which came to $1,200 every two weeks after taxes. Suddenly I was making $3,500 every two weeks. I can remember after my first year in Rochester, I think I had $18,000 in the bank. When I was driving home for the summer, I thought, "This is unbelievable. If I play ten years in this league, I'm going to have a hundred grand in the bank. This is going to be phenomenal. I'm set."

After I scored a goal in my first game, fans noticed me. People started talking about me a little bit. Then I got some more attention because it didn't take long for me to get my first fight—four games. It was with Nevin Markwart of the Bruins. The fight was right in front of our bench at the Aud in Buffalo. I hit him, and he went down and separated his shoulder. Afterward, everyone was talking about how tough the guy was supposed to be. I said, "That guy was tough? He was just a little guy." He was smaller than I was.

I played 27 games for the Sabres that year, but I did a lot of sitting that season. I was scratched from the lineup often. The team was going really good then. We lost one game from the end of October to the end of November, but even that didn't help my mood. Instead, I thought, "OK, maybe the team is going good again. Guys are playing well again. There's no need for me. They're going to send me back down."

To make it worse, even on the nights I played, I didn't get a lot of ice time. I didn't really understand that. I thought, "Why am I not playing?" I got so worked up and frustrated. And I really didn't have anyone to turn to and ask about it … or I was afraid to ask about it, because I didn't want to give the impression that I was bitching. So I just sort of sloughed it off and came back the next day.

I finally was sent back to Rochester in mid-December and stayed there for most of the rest of the season. My attitude when I was sent down was still pretty good. What's the line about life in the minors looking a lot better on the way up than on the way down? That's certainly true.

Once we got done with that season, I thought I had a great chance to go up to the NHL for good. Maguire was traded in March of 1990 for Jay Wells, so I thought there was a spot for me. And as it turned out, I was almost done with the minors.

6

DUDS

In the fall of 1990, I figured it was up to me whether I made the NHL that season. I felt pretty good about my chances. Having played in the league for a while the year before, I had built some some confidence. I was in great shape, and I was anxious to make a good impression right from the start. I could tell the Sabres were taking a long look at me at training camp. They were playing me in exhibition games and using me with better players in practices. The organization's front-office members made more contact with me instead of just saying hello when they walked by.

I suited up for the Sabres on opening night against the Montreal Canadiens and then went down to Rochester. I played eight games there and waited to see what would happen. After the Sabres finally cleared out some roster space for me, I came up for good. There was one big difference on the roster from the previous season. The Sabres had lost in the first round of the playoffs to Montreal the previous spring, and Buffalo traded Phil Housley to Winnipeg for Dale Hawerchuk on draft day.

I was in awe of Hawerchuk. Dale seemed happy to leave Winnipeg, where he was such a star, and come to Buffalo and just play. Doug Gilmour was kind of like that when he came to Buffalo later on. Doug was expected to be great every night in Toronto, but he knew Dominik Hasek would get all the headlines and attention in Buffalo. Dave Andreychuk was a lot more relaxed his second time here too. The expectations on Dave's return were so low that everyone was happy when he got his 20 goals. It's a nice way for these guys to conclude their careers.

Players like Hawerchuk and Andreychuk were so good that I'd ask myself, "Are they looking at me and asking what the heck I'm doing here?" I treaded lightly to see how everyone reacted to me. I started to get to know Rick Dudley, the coach, much better then. I can remember Duds called me to the back of the plane one night shortly after I came back up. He was angry about the way the team was playing.

"Who do you want to play with?" he growled through clenched teeth.

"What?"

"Who do you want to play with?"

"Turgeon and Mogilny," I said off the top of my head.

"OK. Get out of here."

I walked back to my seat and said to someone, "You won't believe what he just said to me."

Two games later, I played with Pierre and Alex. "This is sweet. I should have said something a long time ago," I said. I got to play with them for a fair bit of time and wound up with 16 points, which statistically was my best season. It was great to play with guys like that. All I had to do was get Alex the puck and let him go. I had a pretty simple job—just make sure nobody hit him and try to keep up with him. It didn't last very long, but at least I had a pretty regular shift back then, which was nice.

Once Duds left, I never had that sort of role again. The reduced ice time really showed in my stats. People said, "You don't get the points." Well, I needed to play. Anyone can score a little if they get the playing time.

As you can imagine, I think Duds is a great guy, but he had a difficult time relating to the stars. His motivational methods would have people saying to themselves, "He's picking on me. He's got something against me." They'd think he was a little wacko. But he had to be. He coached the same way he played—with everything he had. He did what he had to do to win, and he worked harder in practice than a lot of players did. Duds taught his players a good work ethic and respect. If you didn't show respect, he'd let you know about it. I related to him pretty well, and I learned a lot from him.

Duds was kind of a philosopher. One on one, he could communicate with someone away from the game. During the game, though, he'd become so intense that communication was tough for him. Some of us knew exactly what he was trying to say, but not everyone can read a person like that. The Knoxes would always be angry about how Duds would act on the bench. He'd yell and scream and pound on the walls. He said to me umpteen times, "If I get carried away, let me know." Then, every night I'd say, "Duds … Duds … relax." He'd say, "Oh yeah, right."

He always carried a New Haven Nighthawks pen, and he always took notes. Sometimes Duds would chew on that pen. One night I turned around to tell him to calm down, and he had blue ink running down the corner of his mouth. I tried to have Rip Simonick, our equipment manager, tell him. "You tell him. I'm not telling him," Rip said.

Finally I said to Duds, "You've got something on your face."

"Oh, oh, oh. OK."

You could tell he cared about winning, and cared about every player in the dressing room. Even in the summer, he worked out with players at Sabreland. When he was away from the rink, he was like a teddy bear. But while he was coaching, he was "Grrrrrrrrrrrrr." You wouldn't have believed the transformation.

That team thought it had a chance to go places, but it never got going. We were on a five-game losing streak when the team had its annual Christmas skating party at the Aud. We had a practice that morning, and families were coming down after that. We were all sitting in the dressing room when we heard Mike Foligno had been traded to Toronto.

We were so shaken about the trade that no one even asked what we had gotten for our captain. We were just shocked that Mike had been traded, and it ticked a lot of guys off. They held a grudge against the team for a long time. Mike was close to the end of his career, but they couldn't figure out why he should be traded for Lou Franceschetti and Brian Curran, especially at that time of the year. Why not keep him around for the rest of the season? It was hard to look at it as "just business."

I've gotten close to a lot of guys who were traded over the years— Matthew Barnaby, Brad May, Ken Sutton. The way I saw it, they were still my friends; they'd just gone somewhere else to work. I would talk to them all the time and see them in the summer. It's a downer at the time, but you have to say, "It's time to go back to work." We had to get over it, although in the case of Mike, it took quite a while.

The trade didn't help us, as we still stumbled along at .500 for the rest of the season. In the next-to-last home game, Guy Lafleur played his last game in Buffalo. It was always a big thrill to play against a guy like that. I think the way the kids think about the legends today is one of the biggest differences in the game since I came up. One time around 2001, Lindy Ruff and I were talking in New Jersey. I told Lindy how that morning Larry Robinson, the coach of the Devils and a Hall of Famer, had said hello to me. One time I had given Robinson a big hit into the boards when he was with Los Angeles, and I thought I had gained respect in his eyes because of it.

"Here I am, 32 years old, and I'm getting excited because Larry Robinson said hello to me, and he's the coach of the other team. Is that right?" I asked.

Lindy laughed and said, "Well, that's respect."

He was right. Guys today don't have respect. There were guys on our team who didn't know who Larry Robinson was.

But some of them sure could put up some numbers. Hawerchuk, Turgeon, Andreychuk, and Mogilny all had at least 30 goals. So we thought we could score some goals in the first round of the playoffs against Montreal, and we did. But we were in no frame of mind to play as a team.

Duds had us get together in the hotel in Montreal. We got in a circle, and he made us go around and tell everybody what each person liked and disliked about all of his teammates. Guys would say, "You're a good guy ... I don't have any problem with you ... You're selfish." I came out of it all right, at least. It was supposed to bring us together, I guess, but we walked out of that room wanting to kill each other. We were done for the playoffs right there.

The games were wide open. The scores of the first four games were 7–5, 5–4, 5–4, and 6–4. I had the game-winning goal in Game Four. I put a wrist shot up top on Patrick Roy. Russ Courtnall scored in overtime to beat us in Montreal in Game Five. Then in Game Six, we were down, 3–1, after two periods. During the intermission, owner Seymour Knox came in and talked to us. That was about the only time I ever saw him upset. He told us how we weren't doing what we were paid to do, that we had a responsibility. Everyone kind of thought, "OK, whatever." He was one of those men that when he got upset, you just shook your head. It was not his role to yell. It was out of character, almost like someone had pressured him into it. Seymour would usually come into the room after a game and just talk about everything but the game.

We gave up a short-handed goal right at the start of the third period, which wrapped it up. The game got so nasty that Canadiens coach Pat Burns pulled Roy because he was afraid Roy would get hurt. Back then, when you knew you were going to lose a playoff series, it would turn into a fight-fest. Leave an impression. Now, guys just quit and get it over with.

During the summer of 1991, the Sabres hired John Muckler as director of hockey operations. John had been the Edmonton Oilers' head coach, and he was an assistant on the great Oilers teams of the 1980s. Muckler later said he was told he would eventually be the team's general manager, although to this day I think it was in the back of his mind that he still wanted to coach. I can remember to this day Duds saying that the two of them didn't see eye to eye from Day One. There was a conflict right from the beginning.

The players figured there would be trades coming after the playoff loss, and they came after the 1991-92 season started. We got Dave McLlwain and Gord Donnelly in a five-man deal with Winnipeg. About two weeks later, we made one of the biggest trades in the history of the franchise. We picked up Pat LaFontaine, Randy Wood, and Randy Hillier for Pierre Turgeon, Uwe Krupp, Benoit Hogue, and McLlwain.

That was quite a change in the roster, and I don't think the Sabres front office was too worried about the chemistry of the team.

I think they just looked at the players they were getting. Nowadays they worry more about what sort of person a guy is.

We were all pretty excited about getting Patty. He was a pretty big name and a pretty good competitor. The guys looked forward to him coming. It didn't take long for him to try to put his stamp on things.

I think the arrival of LaFontaine and Muckler brought the Sabres into the twentieth century. The club was a pretty small operation for a long time—"My buddy does this. My other buddy does that." After the trade, we started to travel better. The dressing room was altered to make it bigger. Medical care improved. It became more of a first-class operation. Muckler and LaFontaine brought new life and new ideas to an old place.

That was right about the time that the NHL was becoming a much bigger business, so it was appropriate that the Sabres stopped being a "mom and pop" organization. Seymour and Norty Knox had to change the way they ran the team. The word *hobby* might be too strong a word to describe how it was run, but in hindsight that's almost what it was like. The Sabres had to stop being content with just making the playoffs; they had to look further ahead.

It was about then that I started to realize why the Sabres had never won anything in the first 21 years of their existence. I started to listen to guys who had played for other teams, and I heard about everything that went on there. My reaction usually was "Wow, that's never happened here." I never knew the difference before. Once new faces came in from outside the organization, they brought in plenty of energy and ideas. Muckler brought a lot here. There was more to the game than what we had been seeing for the previous umpteen years. Nobody had wanted to step on anyone's toes before, but suddenly things were getting done. There was some resistance to change at first, but it faded. It was time to take it to the next level, like the rest of the league had already done.

The new roster took some time to come together, and it was really too late to save Duds. We had gone seven games without a win going into a home game against St. Louis on December 11. Duds knew that night that he was done. He came into the locker room at the end of the first period, and he just went nuts. Everyone got the hint that something was going on, and we all started to feel for him.

We lost the game, 6–3, and the capper was when Brad Miller, one of our own defensemen, scored on our own goalie, Tom Draper. Brad tried to clear the puck, and he put it in the top shelf of the net. Everyone on the bench just exhaled and thought, "It can't get any worse." That took away the last bit of air that Duds had in him. He threw his hands up and thought to himself, that's it. He came in after the game and said more or less that he was done. That sucked, because guys liked him. He never got a lot of help.

Duds never coached in the NHL again. He was a coach in Detroit in the minors, and I talked with some of the players he had there. I think he realized that the stress of coaching was too much for him. Duds thought working in management would be better, and he eventually went on to become general manager in Ottawa, Tampa Bay, and Florida. He works in Chicago's front office now.

***

I saw Duds in the winter of 2001 in Tampa, and I said something I had wanted to say for years. He had just acquired Matthew Barnaby from Pittsburgh in a trade, and I told him what I thought Matthew was all about. When that was done, I shook his hand and said, "I want to thank you. You're the one who gave me my chance, and I appreciate it. If it weren't for you, I wouldn't be standing here now."

He kind of brushed it off and said, "You've done a lot of things right to stay in the league too."

"Maybe, but I might not have been able to have that chance if it hadn't been for you."

He's a tough-act guy who has trouble hearing thanks, but down deep he appreciated it. I respected what he was trying to get from me. There are so many guys who just need an opportunity, and he gave me one.

7

MUCKS

John Muckler walked into the dressing room as the new coach of the Sabres the morning after Rick Dudley was fired to tell us what was going on. Then he said, "I treat superstars like superstars. The rest of you should feel lucky you're here."

I looked around and counted two or three superstars—Pat LaFontaine, Dale Hawerchuk, and maybe Alexander Mogilny. I said to myself, "OK, you're in trouble here." From that point on, Muckler did his own thing. It only took a few days for me to have my first run-in with him, and we had a few more while he was coaching. I've taken out the obscenities in recounting them, but believe me, they were there.

I remember one particularly bad day at practice. Every time I'd make a mistake, I'd swear at myself. I'd say something when I missed a pass or took a shot wide or something and get mad when I screwed up.

Mucks called me aside in the middle of practice and said, "I'm sick of your attitude."

"What do you mean?"

"Every time you screw up you just say, 'Ah, dammit.'"

"Yeah, because I'm mad."

He just started giving it to me after that. I couldn't figure out what it was all about. Every year something would happen and we'd have it out.

One time at Sabreland, Muckler screamed the whole time. "Move the puck. Move the puck. Skate." He never shut up for the whole practice. Finally, he was on one side of the ice and I was on the other side. He was screaming at me, and I stopped dead and yelled back at him.

"If you'd just shut up, everything would be a lot better around here," I said.

"What?"

"You always yell. You're always screaming and yelling at everybody out here, and everybody's so uptight and tense. They can't practice because they're worried about you yelling at them all the time."

"If you don't want to be here, get off the ice."

"I want to be here, but if you'd shut up, everything would be a lot better."

It went back and forth like that. We worked our way to the center of the ice, and we were nose to nose by the time it was over. Everyone was pretty speechless. That was it; nothing was ever said about it again.

The odd part was, I think he respected that I stood up to him at times. But it was tough. My role certainly changed once Mucks took over; I got a lot less ice time. My job was to sit on the end of the bench and then once in a while go out and run around. It was a frustrating living.

Mucks tried to have us play more of an uptempo game the way the Oilers did. We came back a bit toward .500 after he took over, and we made some more trades close to the deadline. Wayne

Presley, Randy Moller, Dave Hannan, and Petr Svoboda all came in during March. We had some talent when all the moves had been made, but were uncertain in goal.

Tom Draper, Clint Malarchuk, and Daren Puppa all played at least 26 games for us that season. In our last regular-season game, Puppa gave up four early goals. Tom Draper came in and shut out Quebec the rest of the way, but it was too late as we lost, 4–3. Mucks decided to go with Draper for the playoff series with Boston.

The playoff series went back and forth. We lost three of the first four games, but Draper won Game Five in Boston with a shutout, and then Patty scored two goals as we won Game Six by 9–3. So it was back to Boston for Game Seven. We had the momentum, but we also had a sense of Buffalo's past playoff failures. The Sabres hadn't won a playoff series since 1983, which had nothing to do with most of us, but we knew all about it. We heard about it every year, starting in March. Most people would count us out of the playoffs before we even got there. And the Sabres had never won a seventh game.

I think before Game Seven guys were saying to themselves, "This is it. This is our year. Things are going for us." The score was tied, 2–2, in the third period, when Boston's Dave Reid skated into our zone and took about a 25-footer from the left side that beat Draper. That was it. Mucks was still angry about that goal years later.

Draper only played 11 more games as a Sabre, as in the summer of 1992 the team tried to improve its goaltending. Buffalo picked up Dominik Hasek from the Chicago Blackhawks in a complicated move; we eventually gave up Christian Ruuttu in the deal. The first time that I ever noticed Hasek was when I saw him that year in the finals. Chicago played Pittsburgh, and Ed Belfour came out in Game Four. Dom came on and stood on his head, even though he gave up four goals on 25 shots. The commentators spent the whole third period talking about him. We didn't know where Dom was going to fit in. We already had Malarchuk, Puppa, and Draper around. We thought Hasek probably would be some sort of backup. Mucks obviously was going to make more changes, as he kept putting his mark on the team.

We didn't worry that much about goaltending in the 1992-93 season. We were too busy scoring, although we were only a little better than .500. We beat Montreal by 8–2, Ottawa by 12–3, Hartford by 8–2 and 9–3, the Rangers by 11–6, and Detroit by 10–7. Seventeen goals in one game—that was a week's work a few years later. We didn't worry about our own end. We just went out and played, going back and forth and hoping our goaltender stopped more than their goalie did.

We sure piled up the stats that season. Mogilny finished with 76 goals. LaFontaine had 148 points. Hawerchuk had 96 points. It was awesome. These guys didn't just go down and score. They left me saying, "Whoa, did you see that?" It was pretty exciting.

Patty and Alex complemented each other extremely well. They both had tremendous speed and they caught some guys off-guard. There were some old defensemen in the NHL who were hanging on at that point. Patty and Alex ate those guys up. Neither one was selfish. It's not like one was trying to avoid setting the other one up, which happens sometimes. I had the odd shift with them to make sure nothing happened to them, and it was fun. I looked at them once and thought, "What am I doing out here?"

Still, we had trouble stopping the other team. On February 1, goalie Grant Fuhr came to Buffalo in a trade. We gave up Puppa, Dave Andreychuk, and a first-round draft choice to Toronto in the deal. The Leafs wanted to move Fuhr because they probably would have lost him in the expansion draft that summer.

We gave up a lot. Puppa was never the same goalie after he broke his arm a couple of years before that, but he wasn't bad. Andreychuk had some great years but was blamed for some of the playoff losses. He was always under pressure, and was a victim. It's easier to move a player and blame him and buy another year of time to solve the problem. But bringing in Fuhrsie was not a bad thing. He did well for us. He gave us more identity and more respect around the league.

We lost our last seven games to finish only a couple of games above .500 for the season. To make matters worse, I hurt my knee against Quebec in one of those losses and missed the entire postseason. I went to hit a guy and caught my foot in a rut. My foot never moved, and my knee bent in half. I stretched one ligament and tore 50 percent of my ACL. I knew something was wrong right away. You might be surprised to know that type of injury doesn't hurt at first. I went back to the bench and decided to go try it during a stoppage of play. I did, and the knee flipped out to the side and went out of control. I knew I was done then. I had arthroscopic surgery, and didn't get back on the ice until July. I was lucky—that was the only major injury I ever had.

It was amazing how quick the procedure is. An hour after surgery, I was riding an exercise bike at the hospital. I went right from the hospital to a therapy center, where I rode the bike some more, iced my knee down, and learned what therapy to use. It was nonstop from there.

Our playoff opponent that spring was again the Boston Bruins, who had guys like Adam Oates, Cam Neely, and Ray Bourque. Patty hurt his knee in Game One, but Bob Sweeney got an overtime goal for us. Two days later, Fuhr got a shutout to give us a sweep of the two games in Boston. We didn't let ourselves think we were about to win a playoff series for the first time in ten years. We were determined to stay on the defensive until it actually happened. Yuri Khmylev scored in overtime in Game Three, and that set up Game Four.

Fuhr was hurt in that game and replaced by Hasek, who played the final 45 minutes. The game went to overtime, and I was standing in one of the walkways behind the bench in order to see how the game ended. Brad May made a couple of fakes, beat Andy Moog, and scored one of the greatest goals in Sabres history to finish the series. That was awesome—not just for us, but for the fans and the organization.

To this day, I can still picture the scene when I walked out of the Aud that night. People were out on the street, blowing their horns and hanging out windows. The hex was off. Ever since then, the Sabres have had pretty good success in the playoffs.

We didn't have much time to celebrate. Patty and Fuhrsie were hurting, and we had to start the next series in Montreal. We lost in four straight, but every game was 4–3, and the last three went to overtime. It's not like we went in and got blown away.

That was a funny year. The brackets for the playoffs opened up, and Montreal wound up beating Los Angeles in the finals. That Sabres team could have gone a long way, particularly if we had stayed healthy. You don't get that many chances at a playoff run.

When we were done, I spent my first full summer in Buffalo working to rehabilitate my knee. An injury like that is a very scary experience to an athlete. Other guys would talk about how long and difficult the recovery process was. Some people never come back from a major knee injury. I asked myself, "Is that going to be me? Am I done?" I just didn't know. A million things went through my mind in a very short period of time. This wasn't even a bad knee injury either.

Meanwhile, Gerry Meehan moved up in the Sabres organization that summer to executive vice-president of sports operations, and Muckler became general manager and coach. When I heard Muckler had done that, I thought I was done. When he took control of player personnel, I figured he'd go get some of his boys from Edmonton that he talked about all the time—guys he felt comfortable with and wanted around.

Muckler made one trade that summer of 1993, getting Craig Simpson from Edmonton. Craig was a good fit for what Mucks was trying to do—go from an Eastern style of play to a Western (more wide-open) style. And that's fine. We did well with it. But he didn't completely change the roster.

We started the 1993-94 season like we had the weight of the world on our shoulders. We lost seven of our first eight. Shortly after that, another ex-Oiler came in when we traded Keith Carney to Chicago for Craig Muni. Craig was known as a big open-ice hitter, and he had a reputation as a mean person on the ice. He was big and played hard, and he did a very good job for us when he came in. He added a dimension to our defense that we didn't really have. We had to give up something to get something, and Keith turned into a decent player, but Craig gave some comfort to a lot of guys out there. He wasn't flashy—get the puck in, get it out. He cleared the front of the net. That's all you could ask for.

We bounced back a little after the slow start, but we got a bad break when LaFontaine's knee didn't heal as well as we'd hoped. Eventually doctors discovered a tear in a ligament, and he was done for the season. That obviously hurt us on the ice, and it had an interesting side effect. Mogilny was named captain of the team—the first Soviet-born captain in NHL history.

Not that he wanted to be captain—he hated the attention. He

just wanted to do his own thing. There was a story making the rounds that the Knoxes liked the idea of making a little history by appointing a Soviet-born captain, and maybe Mucks was trying to give Alex a little more responsibility in an attempt to make him grow a little bit. In a way, it might have been good for Alex—it let him know people wanted him to step up. He didn't want the pressure, but he accepted it.

We got some more bad news in late November when Fuhr was injured. His knee was still bothering him, and the team decided to let him rest and heal completely. That meant Hasek would be the full-time starter for quite a while. At first, that bit of news left the guys feeling nervous. Dom had an unusual style, and he had a different personality from Grant out on the ice. It only took about two games, however, for Dom to show what he could do. Guys looked at what he was doing and said, "Wow." Their attitude totally changed. Dom got back-to-back shutouts in Toronto and Tampa Bay, and was 7-1-1 in his first nine games. He won the team over in record time, and that's very important for a goalie. We had the confidence to go out and play well again. If he had stunk the house out, who knows what would have happened to us that year? Dom went on an unbelievable run, and became the best goalie in the league.

It must have been tough for Grant to be sitting out and watching. The usual line is, "You should never lose your spot in the lineup because of injury." But in a lot of cases, one person's problem is another person's opportunity. Careers are made that way. We had another guy that very season become an established NHL player in that manner. When Patty got hurt, Derek Plante got a chance to move into the regular lineup, and he became a good second-line center for us.

With Patty gone, we changed our style a bit. We switched from the wide-open game to a more defensive game. I remember guys talking about it along the way. It wasn't that difficult, especially since our team then was more suited to a defensive style. It was a lot easier to switch into a defensive mode than it would have been to become a run-and-gun team.

We were pretty steady the rest of that season. We finished sixth in the conference and played the New Jersey Devils in the first round of the playoffs. A lot of people picked the Devils to win the Cup that year, even though they finished second to the Rangers in the regular season.

That was a pretty good series. We split the first four games. I had a goal in Game Four to help us win. I shot from the top of the circle on the right-hand side. I missed the puck a little bit because it was wobbling, and I missed the net, but the puck hit the dasher board and popped straight up. Then it hit the glass and started spinning and came back toward the net. Some people could see the puck was still in play, but Martin Brodeur of the Devils lost sight of it. It hit him on the shoulder, dribbled down his back, and went into the net. That was the oddest goal I've ever scored. People still ask about that one.

After losing Game Five, we came back to Buffalo to play one of the most famous games in Sabre history ... even if I didn't have a big part in it. It took four overtime periods to decide the longest 1–0 game in NHL history.

I got my last shift of the night sometime in the second period. That didn't stop me from getting a ten-minute misconduct before one of the overtime periods. I gave Scott Stevens a little bump as I skated by him, and he gave one back to me. I was happy to get the penalty, if only to sit somewhere else. I was sick of sitting on my own bench by that time. By the second overtime, I started to realize that we were part of something special. Half of the guys wanted to be on the ice to score the big goal, and the other half didn't want to be on the ice because they were afraid of screwing up. Guys talked a lot on the bench, trying to convince their teammates to go out and be a hero.

By the third overtime, I was standing up behind the bench with the coaches to give the guys who were playing some more room. Players were cramping up and vomiting. During the intermissions, the other players were eating bread and drinking orange juice just to get some nutrition in their systems so they could go out and play. As for me, I was in the back room with the trainers, eating chicken wings. I knew I was done for the night. I just wanted to see the game end by then, because I was sick of sitting around. I would have taken my equipment off if I could have gotten away with it.

I remember standing on my stick during the last overtime, just looking around. I turned to Muckler and said, "Hey, Mucks, why don't you give me a chance? Why don't you put me out there? I usually do my best work at this time of the morning."

He looked at me and said, "Not tonight, you're not."

The building was still pretty full when Dave Hannan scored the winner at 1:52 in the morning. It was cool that Dave got the goal instead of one of the big goal-scorers. I played with Dave for quite a while, and he is a good guy. It was the biggest goal of his life, and it was nice to see a guy like him score it.

Dom finished that game with 70 saves in the shutout. After the game, Dom said he could have played maybe one or two more periods. That's how awesome he was. And he showed up for the optional skate the next day. Everyone else was mentally drained and relieved the epic game was over. We had put our skates on at 7 p.m. and taken them off at 2 a.m. It's not like I could go right to sleep when I got home, either.

We had a day off and then had to go right back at it for Game Seven in New Jersey. Both sides played on adrenaline rather than using complicated strategy. New Jersey had a 46–18 edge in shots in the game, but Dom kept it close. He sure made his mark around the league in a short period of time then. Dale Hawerchuk almost tied it in the final minute of regulation, but we ended up losing, 2–1. It hurt to be eliminated, of course, but at least we turned a lot of heads by the way we played.

We didn't make any major moves in the off-season in the summer of 1994. We were all looking forward to the season because a healthy LaFontaine and Simpson figured to be a big help. We went to training camp for a month to prepare, and then we went right back home when the owners called a lockout because of the lack of a collective bargaining agreement. We stayed home until January, when the two sides settled.

We all finally came back to Buffalo for a second training camp. The coaches just hammered us in those first few workouts. They had to get us all in game shape in a very short period of time. The league set up a 48-game schedule, featuring only games within the conference. Those games sucked, because guys weren't in shape. It wasn't very good hockey that year. I also didn't like playing only teams in the East. It was kind of like the old days, when we'd play Hartford eight times a year. That stuff got boring after a while. It would have been nice to play somebody new occasionally.

We opened the season in New York, where we watched the Rangers parade the Stanley Cup around before the game and then beat them. It was Grant Fuhr's last win as a Sabre goalie. He was traded on Valentine Day's to the Kings along with Phillipe Boucher and Denis Tsygurov for Alexei Zhitnik, Charlie Huddy, and Robb Stauber. That worked out great for us. Z was an up-and-coming player, Charlie was a great leader and an awesome guy, and Stauber was a decent backup goalie. We had Hasek, so Fuhr was expendable.

That was a funny season in terms of how we played. We had hot streaks and cold streaks but always stayed a little above .500. Right around the time LaFontaine came back from his knee injury, we lost Dale Hawerchuk to a hip injury. The oddest moment of the season came on March 19, when we lost to Tampa Bay at home by a score of 6–1. After the game, Mucks and assistant coach John Tortorella walked off the ice at the Aud and went by some fans in a small section of gold seats. One fan had been giving it to Mucks whenever he walked by. The fan said something else to Mucks on the way out, and both Muckler and Tortorella slapped at the guy.

We found out later the guy only had one arm and that he worked in the district attorney's office. We heard about it in the locker room.

"Hey, Muckler hit a fan."

"No way."

"And the guy has one arm."

"No Way!"

"Yeah, and he works in the DA's office."

"Oh, he's screwed."

Both coaches got suspended. It was embarrassing, more than anything. It took a long time for Muckler to live that one down. Fans yelled at him around the league about it for quite a while.

A few weeks later I saw a guy in a phone booth find out he had been traded. We took the bus from Boston to Hartford on April 8, which was the day of the trading deadline. Mucks was back in Boston working the phones. When we arrived at the Hartford hotel, assistant coach Don Lever pulled Petr Svoboda into this little room off the lobby that had a pay phone in it, and told him he had been traded to Philadelphia for Garry Galley. At least Petr didn't hear about it on television or through the newspaper. That happens more than you'd think.

A short time later, Ken Sutton was told he'd been traded to Edmonton for Scott Pearson. Sutton went ballistic with the coaches when he found out, saying the Sabres would regret the deal. Then when Sutton came down to talk to the media on his way to the airport, he was as calm as could be and wished the team success. Sutts is a good friend. It wasn't in his nature to go off on the coaches like that, but he did it behind closed doors—where you're supposed to do it. He was frustrated and disappointed about leaving, but he got the last laugh—his name is on the Stanley Cup from his time in New Jersey.

We finished seventh in the regular season, which set us up to play the Philadelphia Flyers in the first round of the playoffs. We lost the first two games, won Game Three, but lost Game Four. I was pretty angry about how the team was reacting to the series at that point, and I gave an emotional interview to the media between Games Four and Five. Players don't understand that when you lose, changes are made and somebody takes the blame. Guys were pointing fingers at each other and accepting the losses as if they were no big deal. "It was the other guy's fault" was the attitude that went around the room.

My little speech didn't help. The Flyers came out and smoked us right from the start of Game Five. We kind of gave up and were never close to winning. We had about a three-hour wait until we got on the plane home, and by the time we actually started flying, guys were already talking about their investments—everything but hockey. Some guys take the attitude that when the game's over, it's over. They don't worry about games that have been played. I'm not saying everyone is like that. It's a handful that say, "So be it," and look at the game as a job, lacking that drive to win. If a guy has a long career but doesn't win a Stanley Cup, is that a successful career? I don't know. Some guys just look at their bank accounts to make that judgment. And it's going to get worse and worse.

We were a fractured team at that point, and many changes had been made by the time we started the next season.

I was on my first hockey team by age three. *Courtesy of Rob Ray*

Learning the ropes as an enforcer was tough when I was playing for Rochester. *Courtesy of the Rochester Americans*

Bill Guerin, shown here in a fight with me when he was with the Devils, can play hockey any way you want to play it. *Photo by Harry Scull Jr.*

Officials often had their hands full when tempers boiled over. *Photo by Harry Scull Jr.*

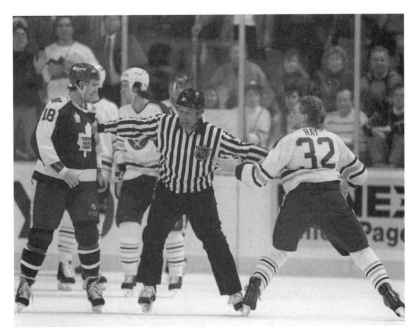

Kevin Maguire and I square off. Kevin later became an NHL linesman. *Photo by Harry Scull Jr.*

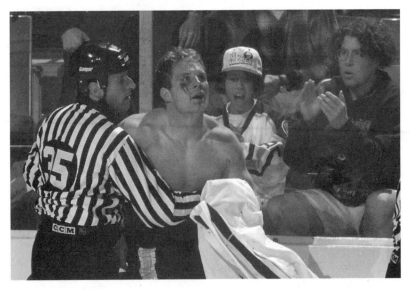

If you think hockey fights are staged, check me out here. *Photo by Harry Scull Jr.*

Another day at the office for me against Calgary. *Photo by Harry Scull Jr.*

Matthew Barnaby (left), me, and Brad May (right) were part of the "hardest working team in hockey" for a few years. *Photo by Harry Scull Jr.*

I watched more than 3,000 minutes of NHL hockey from the penalty box over the years. *Photo by Harry Scull Jr.*

A goal was always cause for celebration, and Mike Foligno joins in here.
Photo by Harry Scull Jr.

Mario Lemieux was a handful to play against—great skill mixed with a chip on his shoulder. *Photo by Harry Scull Jr.*

The 1994-95 Sabres take a little break before going to work. *Photo by Harry Scull Jr.*

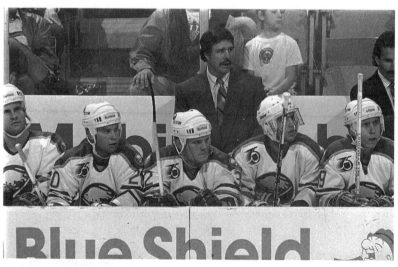

Rick Dudley gave me an opportunity to make it in the NHL. I'll always remember him for that. *Photo by Harry Scull Jr.*

Playing hockey in a physical style didn't just mean I got into fights.
Photo by Harry Scull Jr.

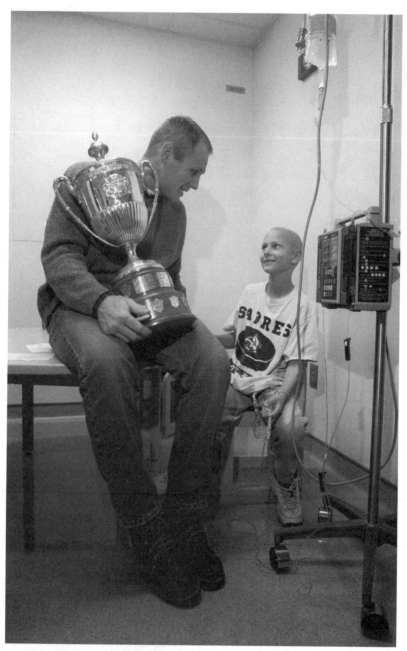

What's the point of winning a trophy if you can't share it with somebody? *Photo by Harry Scull Jr.*

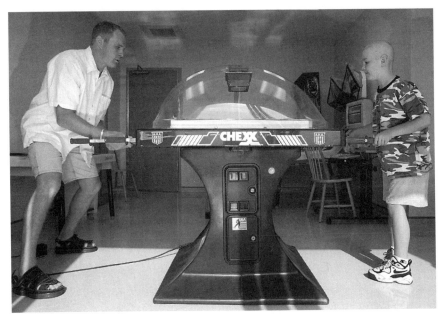

Hospital visits are supposed to cheer the kids up, but I felt better afterward too. *Photo by Harry Scull Jr.*

It's never too early to start on the fundamentals. *Photo by Harry Scull Jr.*

Jay McKee, Steve Shields, and I visit the bowling alleys in the White House. *Courtesy of Budd Bailey*

Posing with assorted members of the Sabres' traveling party on the back lawn of the White House was a thrill. *Courtesy of Budd Bailey*

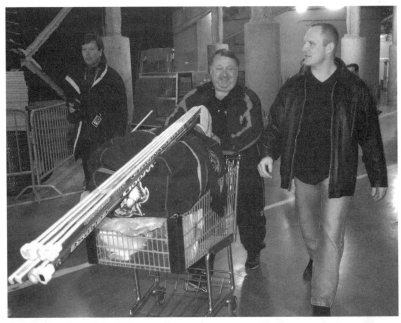

Rip Simonick helps me with my equipment on the day I was traded by the Sabres to Ottawa. *Photo by Harry Scull Jr.*

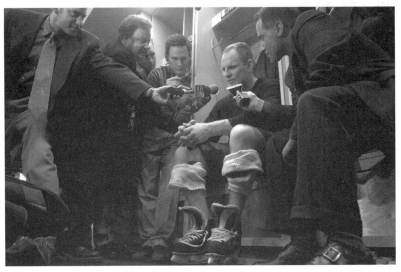

It could get a little crowded in the dressing room when the media wanted to talk to me. *Photo by Harry Scull Jr.*

Thanks for a great ride! *Photo by Harry Scull Jr.*

8

TEDDY AND BARNEY

In the summer of 1995, I became a head coach … although not with the Sabres.

I was the coach of the Buffalo Stampede roller hockey team. I did it as a favor to a group in town that was involved with the team—sponsors, mostly. They thought I could bring a little recognition to the team. It was fun, although it was a little strange. I had played hockey with some of the guys on the roster, and I had a hard time not sending guys over the boards. I kept thinking, "Who am I to say somebody shouldn't play?" I wasn't really prepared to bench players. The only way they got paid was if they played in games, and they were depending on that money. I just didn't want to be the bad guy. I didn't really like the people running the team, but I made a commitment and didn't want to bail out on them. I coached the home games and went on a few road trips, but it really took up too much time from my summer.

It was odd to deal with players who were mostly from the low minors. They were guys who were done with the East Coast Hockey League season and who were looking to pick up a few extra bucks in the summer. It reminded me of the time I went from Buffalo to

Rochester. Buffalo was more professional, a place where guys had separate lives. In the minors, players are together all the time. Their wives are even part of the group. Two, three, or four players live together. It's almost like college, and some of these guys were 30 years old. I'd feel like telling them, "Quit the game, get a job, and enter the real world. Get on with your life." The players were either really young or older guys who didn't want to let go of hockey. I had buddies that played in those low minor leagues all over the world for virtually nothing, and they were content with it. I tried to be supportive with them, but I always dropped in a line like, "When is enough enough? When are we moving into the real world?"

Meanwhile, the Sabres cleaned house in the summer of 1995. President Doug Moss had told John Muckler to cut the payroll. Alexander Mogilny was traded to Vancouver for three prospects, and Dale Hawerchuk and Wayne Presley were allowed to walk away as free agents. It was like starting over, saying the first attempt at building a team didn't work. It was a smart move on Muckler's part. In addition, Mucks became a full-time general manager and gave up his coaching duties.

Ted Nolan was hired to coach the team. I still followed junior hockey when I was in the NHL, and Teddy's name came up quite often for the job he did coaching in Sault Ste. Marie. I met him for the first time before training camp, but we didn't have a long talk. I didn't want to throw myself at the new coach.

Teddy was very welcome in our dressing room that fall because he had such a different approach from Muckler. He brought a different feeling to the team and to the dressing room, especially once we got to know each other. Teddy didn't treat anyone differently than anyone else. He didn't care if you were a one-day pro or a 20-year pro. I think that's why guys respected him. Players liked the type of person he was. He made us work hard, but he wasn't intimidating. He was more apt to sit and talk to you as a buddy. Teddy had the best relationship with players of any coach I've ever had.

Teddy had a whole new team. Michael Peca came over in the Mogilny trade. Brian Holzinger, Brad May, and Jason Dawe got larger roles. We had a young, eager roster, and Ted was used to dealing with young players from his days in junior. He could really relate to that team.

One guy who got his first full shot at the NHL that year was Matthew Barnaby, one of the most memorable characters of my career. When Barney first came to Buffalo a few years before that, I got a call from Mucks: "Look, we've got a guy coming into camp this fall named Matthew Barnaby. I don't want you fighting him." OK, no big deal. First few days of camp, I played against Barney and he started chasing me all over the rink. He did everything possible to start something. Finally, I said the heck with this, and we fought. At the end, his gloves were by my feet. Stupidly, he bent down right in front of me to pick up his gloves. Just as he did that, I suckered with an uppercut and lifted him up and then skated away. We fought again later on.

He is misunderstood, but I got to know him and learned about his background. He went through a lot as a kid: his father left him at a young age, and his mother and his brother raised him. To this day, he puts his mother and brother on a pedestal. But Matthew has always had a chip on his shoulder. He'd say, "I'm going to prove everyone wrong. I'm not too small," and I think that has driven him to get to the NHL.

I can say that I know what kind of person he is away from the game too. He is unbelievably nice to my family, and every time we talk, he asks, "How's your mom and dad?" We became close friends. I probably talk to Matthew on the phone more than anybody, just about life in general. And when his mother-in-law died in 2000, I was a pallbearer at the funeral. I consider his family my family and spend a lot of time with them. A lot of people would never believe that by how we act on the ice, but when it's over, it's over.

In 1995, I saw him as a guy who was usually out of control and living life on the edge. I was just moving out of that stage, and I tried to pass on a little advice. Of course, I'd never listen when anyone told me anything at that age, and neither did he. Matthew would say and do things that would make me say, "What are you doing? Why are you doing this?" We argued and fought all the time. It wasn't a bad relationship, but that was the way we dealt with things.

Matthew thrives on attention. He'd say, "Any attention, good or bad, is awesome." That's why I like him. He doesn't try to be someone he's not. He doesn't say things to please people. He says what's on his mind. He gets himself in trouble, but he deals with the consequences. When he messes up, he's the first one to admit it.

Matthew became a regular in 1995-96 and had the first of two good years under Teddy. In fact, Teddy got more out of Matthew than any other coach. I think it was because Teddy treated him with respect. Teddy understood Matthew and knew where he came from and what he had to do to get there. Teddy showed a lot of faith in Matthew, and Matthew fed off of that. For the first time, someone in a power position had put a lot of faith in Matthew and made him feel like he was a big part of the team. Matthew felt like he deserved to be there, and in return Matthew respected Teddy more than anyone else. I think maybe Teddy became a father figure to him. Matt might have been close to going back to Rochester around then, but Ted came along at just the right time. Ted said, "This is the way it is. This is your responsibility. You're part of this team," and it brought him around.

It was an odd season. We did all right, and were on the edge of playoff contention. The bodies came and went throughout the season as Muckler continued to make moves. We picked up two players and two draft choices from San Jose for Doug Bodger. I was sorry to see Doug go. He was a good guy and could be a bit of a character.

One time in the early '90s, I remember we were down a goal at home when Doug came off the ice with about a minute left. Mucks said, "What are you doing? Get back out there!"

Doug replied, "I'm tired!"

Another time, Doug was deathly ill and shouldn't have been near the rink. The trainer told Mucks that he didn't think Doug could play, and Mucks said, "What do you mean? Tell him to get in here."

Doug walked in. Mucks asked him, "Can you play?"

"Boy, I don't know. I'm dying. I'm really sick," Doug answered.

"You can't play a regular shift?"

"I don't think so."

"Think you could play on the power play?"

"Well, I might be able to play the odd power play."

"You're playing."

Doug wound up playing a regular shift for the entire game. He reminded me a little of Alex Zhitnik—always smiling, never had a bad day. It didn't matter what was happening, he always found the positive side of life. He was a fun guy to be around and a heck of a player.

In December, we had a run of injuries to our goaltenders as both Dominik Hasek and Andrei Trefilov were lost for a while. We had to recall Martin Biron from junior hockey, our first-round draft choice.

He got to play in his first NHL game against the Pittsburgh Penguins, who had Mario Lemieux, Jaromir Jagr, and Ron Francis. We were all sitting around laughing at him before the game. "Get ready, because here they come," we said. We thought Lemieux and Jagr were going to kill this kid. He had been talking before the game about how excited he was to face the Penguins, but we all wondered how excited he'd be after the game. We knew we were in trouble before we took the ice. Sure enough, they got a few very quickly in the first period. It was a reality check for Marty.

Marty hung around for a while even though we signed John Blue to help us out in goal. We went up to Montreal several days after the Pittsburgh game. Blue started the game, and Marty was on the bench. I think that was the first time I ever saw a guy do an interview from the bench during the game. There was Marty, talking away to *Hockey Night in Canada*. He never shut up. Marty went into the game later on, and we won, 7–6.

We saw the tough side of Teddy a few weeks later in Florida. The Panthers blew us out on a Saturday night. We were supposed to have Sunday off, but after the game Ted told us, "No day off—practice here tomorrow." The guys were very ticked off about it. On Sunday, we got on the ice and started skating around and around and around. After a while we started wondering when we'd actually start practicing. We skated for 20 minutes, and then Ted told us to shoot on the goalies. We did that for ten minutes, and then it was back to skating around. We skated around and around. We followed that pattern—20 minutes of skating, ten minutes of drills. At the end, we all gathered by the boards, and in a voice that could be heard throughout the Miami Arena, Ted said, "You wasted my time last night, so I wasted yours today."

The Florida game was part of a slump that dropped us seven

games under .500 at the end of January. We picked up Bob Boughner from Florida, and he was part of a whole new image for the team. We had Boogie, Brad May, and Matthew to go with me. Teddy liked a rough style of hockey, and it was nice to have so many guys who could play that way. It didn't matter who was on the ice at a given moment. We had someone coming at the other team almost all the time. When things got bad, he could throw us all out there. Teams didn't want to play us back then. I've talked to guys who faced us, and they say, "We used to hate playing you guys." Our tactic served its purpose. It gave a lot of young guys confidence.

But we didn't come too close to making the playoffs, and by the end of March, the countdown was on to the end of the season. Still, we were getting ready to move into the new building a block away, and to accompany the move, the club decided to unveil new uniforms. The players had been shown a hundred different design combinations, but we just wondered how the change would go over. On April 11, we had an open practice for the debut of our new uniforms, and the players all thought, "What are we doing? No one is going to come to a practice." But Memorial Auditorium was filled, and they had to turn 5,000 people away. We couldn't believe it.

Three days later, we played the last game of the season and the last game ever in the Aud. I knew the day was coming, of course, but it's always sad to see an old building after the team moves out. One time we practiced in the Forum in Montreal after the Canadiens had left for the Molson Centre. Pieces of glass were missing, seats were missing, and stuff had been ripped down. That building had so much history, and it was being demolished. You can never replace that stuff. You might have the pictures and videos, but it's not the same.

I knew everyone in the Aud, from the guy who was in charge of the lot where I parked to the guys who cleaned the ice. I used to love to sit in Rip Simonick's equipment room down in the basement. Everyone who ever played in Buffalo would congregate there. You couldn't sit and talk in the hallway, but you could do it there. Guys from other teams also showed up. Sometimes the vendors and souvenir guys and the Zamboni drivers would be there. It's a whole different feeling with the new building. I walk in and see the security guards in the back, but I never see the vendors and the ushers. We're taken away from all of these people.

Appropriately, I got kicked out of that last game. I can remember going into the dressing room late in the second period. All the alumni guys who were involved in the postgame ceremony were sitting around. I sat there with those guys, having a beer and talking. Then all of a sudden I had to go back on the ice for the ceremonies. That was a little tough.

After I had changed into street clothes, I went up to the concession stand at the front of the building—"The Poor Man's Aud Club," we called it—and had a beer. I used to do that a lot after home games. I realized that it would be the last time I'd ever be in the building. And as I made my final exit, I saw people who didn't want to leave still sitting in their seats. I knew how they felt.

9

DIVISION CHAMPS

The 1996-97 season is a difficult one to explain. There were so many different things that went on that it hit a point where no one knew whom to believe, whom to trust. There were many internal battles going on in the front office, and it got so bad that guys on the team wouldn't even look at each other and talk to each other, because we didn't know whom we could talk to without it getting back to someone else.

It was not fun. Yet in spite of all that, we went from being out of the playoffs to division champions in a year. I never had a season like it.

When I just thought about hockey in the summer of 1996, I felt pretty good about the team. We had brought in a lot of good young players the previous year—Michael Peca, Matthew Barnaby, Brian Holzinger, Mike Wilson—and more were on the way, like Curtis Brown. We thought we had the makings of a good team. Maybe we didn't think we'd be great in 1996-97, but we had the potential to do well down the road.

Meanwhile, Muckler and Nolan were getting ready for their second year together. When Teddy came here to be coach, I think

Mucks thought in the back of his mind that Teddy would be happy to be there and would let the manager call all the shots. I think that happened for the first little while. When the team started playing well for Teddy—he knew the players as well as anyone, and he was making good decisions—the conflict grew.

During that summer, Seymour Knox III passed away, which was sad. We could have used him in the months to come; maybe he could have helped get everyone together on the same page.

I've talked to a lot of guys on different teams around the league, and sometimes they had never even met their owners, who might show up once a year. Seymour and Norty, his brother, would come in after a win—never after a loss, because they knew it wasn't the time—and they'd shake everyone's hand. They made you feel like a member of one big happy family. When I first got to the Sabres, I thought that was pretty cool. Here's the owner of the team, asking how my mom and dad are and how things are at home. It gave a pretty nice feeling to the players. They were almost too nice to everyone.

To this day, when I see Jean Knox (Seymour's wife) or Seymour IV, they still say hello. I know them more than just as people who used to own the team. They're friends. I wouldn't hesitate for a second to call Mrs. Knox if I needed something, because she'd be the first one to help.

It's too bad Seymour never got to see the new building completed, because that really added to the excitement everyone felt for the 1996-97 season. The new arena was going to be state of the art, and it was one of the biggest things to happen to Buffalo in years. In the summer, when the players would take tours of the new place, we wouldn't care about anything else in the arena other than the dressing room. It was so big. I found myself saying, "What are

they going to put in here? What are they going to put over there?"
The only NHL home locker room I had been in was the one in the
Aud, where everything was tightly confined. In the new place,
everyone had his own individual stalls in a dressing area. There was
a lounge. There was a sauna. I felt like I had joined a country club.
It was phenomenal.

After a couple of weeks of training camp, we got to play in our
first game in Marine Midland Arena on September 21. The first
night, when everything was done and the carpeting was in, I just
looked around and said, "Wow." The medical room was great. The
weight room was great. I felt like I could spend a whole day there.
Everything was top notch. It's still one of the best in the league, even
though there have been other new buildings finished around the
league since then.

I don't know how much people were "into" those first few home
games, especially in preseason. The fans were looking at the
Jumbotron, walking around, seeing what was there. Sometimes
people weren't even in their seats during play because they were
checking everything out. There was a transition period. I think
everyone was in awe.

We played like we were in a transition period, too. We lost two of
our first three in Western Canada, came back home to play the first
regular-season game in the new place, and got blasted by Detroit,
6–1. Then a few nights later at home, Pat LaFontaine skated into the
Pittsburgh zone and got caught in the head with an elbow from
Francois Leroux of the Penguins. Patty had to be helped off the ice
and didn't return to the game. So were 1-4 at that point, were
playing a good Pittsburgh team, and our captain was going to be out
for a while. The fans must have been thinking, "Oh, oh."

We were more worried about LaFontaine than the team at that

point. Patty had missed a lot of playing time in the preceding few years, so the team knew how to play without him. Guys knew they had to step up when they got more playing time and more responsibility. Star players want to be on the ice all the time. They want to be out there every other shift. Some coaches will play their stars like that. They'll have a set line for a star and then throw him out with another line every so often to get him out as much as possible.

I don't want to ever say having a player get hurt is good for a team. Patty went through hell with it. But the guys looked at each other and said, "We've got to pick it up," and we started playing a lot better. We beat Pittsburgh the night of LaFontaine's injury and went on a winning streak, and Patty started playing again in about a week.

Patty continued to play through early November, but he wasn't the same guy. You could see it in his eyes. Sometimes I like to look into a player's eyes before the game and ask, "Are you ready?" If he's ready, you can see it there. That's the best place to judge. Too many times I'd look at Patty and he had a lost look in his face. His eyes would go in different directions.

I've seen that look with other guys. I've had it. You're light-headed. Then in a few weeks or a month, you wake up one day and feel good. The feeling almost vanishes. The fog blows away.

Patty was told on November 8 to take a week off, and that stretched into a few months when doctors diagnosed the effects of the concussion. Patty was a guy who needed to be on the ice all the time; the more he played, the better he was. But the postconcussion syndrome developed to the point where it was no big deal to him if he didn't play. And I think that scared him. He didn't know what was going on.

He brought a lot of attention to the concussion problems of the sport. I know by the end of that year guys were taking tests. Before Patty's injury, everyone got concussions and it was no big deal. Players would tell their roommates not to let them sleep for too long. The next day, they'd come to the rink, take a couple of aspirin, and away they'd go. So many guys were hurt, and nobody ever knew it. But when something like that happens to a player like Patty, it calls attention to it. People want to know what happened.

My last concussion was in 1998-99 from a fight with Stu Grimson in Anaheim. I didn't think it was any big deal at the time. All of a sudden, the next night we played in Los Angeles. I went out in warm-ups, took three strides, turned ... and fell. My balance was gone. I couldn't stand up. It didn't matter what I did—as soon as my blood started circulating, I lost it.

I've had about six concussions in my life, and I started to worry about them a lot more at the end of my career. I thought back to what happened over the years. Paul Kruse, my teammate, hit me the same year. We were going after the same guy, and he came across and hit me with an elbow by mistake. I was knocked senseless. I couldn't even get to the bench. Then a doctor asked if this had ever happened before, and I said, "Four or five times." The doctor said, "Are you serious?" Well, no one ever made a big deal out of it before.

Patty announced on November 15 he would be out indefinitely because of the injury. The next day, we were supposed to play the Bruins at home. I went to the morning practice and went home for lunch. I took a nap until 3:30 p.m. All of a sudden the phone started ringing.

"Did you hear?"

"What?"

"The Jumbotron collapsed."

"Come on. No way. What are you talking about?"

Then someone from the team called to tell me not to come in, because the Jumbotron had fallen to the ice and the game was canceled. My first thought: "We just got off the ice and that thing fell!" I didn't know much about it. I found out later no one is allowed under the scoreboard when it's being moved, just in case something like that happened.

I didn't think it could happen with a new arena—I had to drive down just to check it out. When I got there, I could not believe it when I saw the pile of debris. It was funny, and I had never seen anything like it. The front office was almost in shock: "My God, the Jumbotron fell." The team was lucky that nothing underneath broke when the scoreboard collapsed. I can't imagine how heavy that thing is. You'd think some pipes would have been broken.

Once they got a new one back up, it became something of a running joke: "Don't skate under the Jumbotron." Everyone was looking up at it at practice, going wide along the boards instead of skating down the middle of the ice.

We got pretty hot after that and moved around the top of the Northeast Division. Dominik was playing so well that we just wanted to ride the wave. At the time, everyone talked about how good he was, and the rest of us thought, "If we ever get our act together, how good could we be?" It was such a good feeling. We were all so excited.

Even when we didn't win, we got a lift from Dom. We played a 0–0 tie in New Jersey on December 23 in which both Hasek and Martin Brodeur had thirty-seven saves. At the end of the game, no one could figure out who should get the puck for the shutout. They wound up cutting the puck, and each goalie kept half. They both deserved it.

And the funny part was that while everything was getting better and better on the ice, the situation off the ice was deteriorating quickly. I heard Muckler had gone to team president Larry Quinn at some point early in the year and said he wanted to fire Nolan, and Quinn said Muckler had to take over as coach if he wanted to do that. Muckler wanted Don Lever as head coach, so he wouldn't do it.

Normally, all of this would be no big deal to the players. We still had to go out and play and do what was expected. The problem was that everyone was talking. Both guys were trying to get players on this side for support. They'd pull players aside and say, "This is what's going on" and "He's trying to do this." Then the next guy would come along and tell you a different story. Then a third guy would tell you something totally different, or half and half. You didn't know whom to believe.

Yet we kept winning and clinched a playoff spot on March 21 with a win in Washington. It was around that time that Muckler came in and more or less told us, "Don't be content with just making the playoffs. You've got to do something when you get there." I think it was a smart move, even though I think the coaching staff thought it made the team too nervous and resented the interference. Their attitude was, "Things are going good. Why put that added pressure on us?" But Muckler told us early enough that we had enough time to loosen up and realize what he was talking about. I give Muckler a lot of credit for moves like that. He was smart that way. He knew what buttons to push to get guys going.

Even so, we stumbled along a bit after that as we closed in on the division title. On April 9 in Boston, Dominik didn't think practice was tough enough and he just blew up. He left the ice, trashed the locker room, and was gone. At the time, nobody knew what was going on. "What was that for?" we all said.

I knew there was the possibility for problems between Dominik and Teddy. One time in Florida, Dom and Alexei Zhitnik and maybe one other guy—all Europeans—were late for practice. Teddy wouldn't allow them on the ice. When practice was over, he yelled at us. Then, all of a sudden, Teddy said, "You [bleeping] Europeans. You come over here and you don't respect what you've got. You don't know what's given to you." We all said, "Huh?" It was a five-second outburst and it was over. But from that point on, things were never the same.

It was totally out of character for Teddy. I don't know if he got caught up in the moment that he didn't know what he was saying. And Teddy, being part of the Native community, is the one guy who knows all about stereotypes and prejudice. That's why people couldn't understand why he ever said it. I still don't.

After our light practice at the FleetCenter, we got the dressing room cleaned up after Dom's rampage, and there was some talk in the media that day that Dom and Teddy weren't getting along. I didn't think it was that serious at the time. The next night we beat Boston, 5–1, to win the division title. We were in control the whole way. With about a minute left, Teddy came up to Garry Galley, Zhitnik, Donald Audette, Brad May, and me after a whistle. "You guys have been here the longest. You guys got us here. You guys are going to finish it off," Nolan said to us.

I just turned around and said, "Really?" That was pretty cool. For him to think of it and actually go through with it was really nice. He thought enough of the players to do that. That's the kind of guy Teddy was—he always made you feel like you were a part of the team. He probably was the first coach I ever had who treated us with enough respect, and that's why guys liked to play for him and liked him so much. That's why he did what he was able to do. He demanded respect in return, but he still treated us like grown men even though we were a young team. I think guys realized that and played hard.

When the buzzer went off, the Sabres were division champions for the first time since 1981. That was an awfully good feeling. For the young guys, it was really good for them to know what it was like to win. They learned what the game was all about.

We went from a team that didn't get much attention to a team that caused a stir around town. That was the most exciting time I had had in several years. I was proud to walk around town and say I was part of the team. Some years before, I kind of buried my face and said in a low voice, "Yeah, I'm part of the team."

If you look at that team, it's kind of amazing what we accomplished. The leading scorers were Derek Plante and Brian Holzinger. Donald Audette led the team in goals. Jason Dawe and Matthew Barnaby had great years. Most of them were never better than they were that year. I was on more talented Sabres teams, but this was the one that won the division. Sure, Dominik was phenomenal and deserves a lot of credit, but Teddy put the pieces together.

The atmosphere around us as we got ready for the playoffs was amazing. No one had the slightest idea what was going to happen next. A bunch of us got together for dinner shortly before the start of the series with Ottawa, and one of the guys said, "I bet you Dom doesn't last the series." Most people at the table said, "What are you talking about?" Some of the players believed Dom was going to "pull the chute," or quit on the team. We talked about it for a while, and that was typical of what was going on. Too many guys had too many things on their minds before we started the playoffs. I thought Dom was way too much of a competitor to pull the chute over anything.

Why do what we did all year to quit in the playoffs? I just thought it was crap, and I felt badly for Dom.

We split the first two games of the series with the Senators at home and went to Ottawa for Game Three. We were up, 1–0, in the second period of Game Three when a shot was deflected by Hasek and into the net. Dom immediately fell to his back in apparent pain. He got up, flexed his leg, and skated directly to the Sabres bench. He then walked up the runway to the locker room, and Steve Shields came in to replace him.

I was sitting on the bench, and that little dinner conversation we had just popped back into my head. "No ... no." As I said, there were so many things in people's heads that when something did happen, people got suspicious. The action made guys wonder even more. There are no doctors on the team. The players don't know how to diagnose an injury. It just caused another eruption.

To this day, I still think he was hurt. In the opening game of the 2000-01 season, a guy landed on Dom's knee. It scared him and he got right up and skated to the bench. He just doesn't lie there in that situation. He comes off. That's the way he handles it.

We still won the game. Dom told the media afterwards he felt a pop in his knee and would miss Game Four at the least. The team doctor pronounced him day to day. The next morning was an off-day in the series, but there was plenty to read. Jim Kelley of *The Buffalo News* wrote, "I don't for a moment believe that Dominik Hasek intentionally bailed out on his coach and his teammates Monday night, but I do believe the pressure of having to be unbeatable may well be more than even he can bear. If that's the case, there may be more than a slightly sprained knee to worry about."

Dom carried our team all year. He led us to first place. Even three years later, people would say the Sabres would only go as far as Dom could carry them. It's tough to have that on your shoulders every night. A normal person would have cracked under that pressure, but he didn't. He played, and played well.

After practice before the next game, Dominik briefed the media on his condition. He had a copy of Kelley's column in his hand and answered questions from everyone—including Kelley—quite calmly.

We lost Game Four in overtime and flew back to Buffalo. The next day was another off-day, and Dominik had a news conference to say how much he needed and appreciated the support of his teammates in all of this. Meanwhile, the rest of the players were in the locker room when someone came in and said, "Sit down, we're going to have a press conference." Everyone was like, "What happened now?"

Quinn walked up to me with a piece of paper and said, "Here, you're going to read this."

"Read it for what?" I answered.

I thought I was going to read it to the guys. The next thing I know, there's 50 media people in front of me. I looked down at the paper quickly, shook my head, and thought, "Why do I have to do this? What does it matter?"

I read the statement, which supported Dominik. The next thing I knew, it was being carried on TV all across North America. We always supported Dom, so as long as we knew it in the dressing room I didn't care if anyone else believed it.

The next day, we lost Game Five, 4–1. Right after the game, Dom came out of the locker room, saw Kelley in the hallway, and physically went after him. Dom grabbed Kelley's shirt, and he had to be pulled away by Dawe and another writer. I was still in the locker room when it happened, and I couldn't believe it.

Something sparked Dom that day, because he had been fine with Kelley a couple of days before that. Dom was storming that whole day. I think he was so frustrated and didn't know who to listen to or who to believe, and it all came to a head. I'm not saying it was Jim's fault or Dom's fault; in fact, I think they were both victims. Dom had the pressure of the world on him, not only just because he was the best goalie in the world and the leader of our team, but because things were getting pushed into his head. Dom is not a confrontational type of guy who would normally do something like he did.

Teddy canceled practice the next day, and we all met in a banquet room at the hotel in Ottawa. Teddy took that time to speak his piece. He didn't give a speech to gain support. He just reviewed the situation and said, "This is what's going on. It's between me and Mucks. You guys have nothing to do with it. Don't let what's going on with us interrupt what you guys are here to do. It's our lives, not yours. You're the ones playing, and you might not get this opportunity again. Go do what you've got to do."

He also talked about how he had messed up. "It happened, now let's get on with it," he said. It wasn't a one-sided speech. He didn't say he was God and everyone else was wrong. I thought it was a pretty good speech. It put guys at ease and helped us to understand what was going on.

We got a shutout the next night, 3–0, to force a seventh game. Supposedly Muckler suggested to Nolan that he use Andrei Trefilov in goal for that game, but Teddy stuck with Steve, and his decision paid off. Steve was great. It was his first pro shutout.

Back home, Dom and Jim patched things up a bit the next day. We all could start thinking about the series, and there was a ton of drama there too. The Sabres had never won a Game Seven in history. The team had never even played one at home. In fact, it had won only one playoff series since 1983.

I think all of the tension from the season helped us in Game Seven. We were pretty nonchalant about it. I saw some guys in the Sabre dressing room over the years later that wouldn't have been able to handle it had they been on that team. Most of us had never been in a Game Seven, and we didn't look at it as if it was going to be a major problem. We just played the game.

Even after the game began, the tension continued to rise. Plante floated in a goal off a face-off in the third period to tie the game, and we went to overtime. Then Derek came down the right side, took a shot that tipped off the end of Ron Tugnutt's glove, and dribbled across the goal line for the winning goal.

I was on the bench, and every mouth just opened up to scream. We all piled excitedly onto the ice. The second that celebration ended, I think it hit a lot of guys. "We did it." It was like we had won the Stanley Cup. There was nothing better than that feeling, especially for a young team. That win gave us confidence that helped us in the playoffs for the next two years.

After all that, anything would have been an anticlimax. We went into the second round to play Philadelphia, but the guys had nothing left to give. We had already accomplished what we needed to accomplish. Mentally, the guys were spent. We lost that series in five games.

Afterward, some people still thought we had messed up. "What did you guys do?" they asked. "You shouldn't have lost it." We had overcome a thousand obstacles to get to the second round, and you couldn't expect anything more. That team had given everything it had.

When we were done, I figured we'd have a little peace and quiet to calm down a bit. That didn't turn out to be the case.

10

LINDY

Our team was finally coming together. There was a lot more interest in the Sabres in the area, because of the exciting team we had. I don't know if the 1996-97 team was the most talented team I've ever played on, but it was effective and people liked us. The excitement that was created in the regular season was terrific, and then playing well in the playoffs escalated that to a whole new level. Right after we lost to Philadelphia in the second round, guys were really looking forward to coming back in the fall of 1997 for the new season.

But we didn't know then who would be in the hockey department when we got there. There were so many things that went on in 1996-97. We knew there was a conflict between Ted Nolan and John Muckler. None of the players knew what exactly was going on, but we knew something might happen. We never thought both of them would go.

When Mucks was fired a couple of days after we were eliminated from the playoffs, we all said, "Wow," because everybody considered him one of the greatest minds in the game. He put the team together with guys that jelled and overachieved. We had every aspect of a team that you would need. To get rid of somebody like that made us say, "I wonder what's going on here."

The players worried about who the new general manager might be, because the GM puts the team together. If you're not the type of player that a GM is looking for, the chances of you being moved are pretty good. The coach may have less to say about that. The GM will say, "This is what you've got to work with—go coach it."

I had never heard of Darcy Regier before he got the general manager's job. Even when he coached as an assistant for the Islanders and Whalers, I hadn't noticed him. So when he was hired, my first reaction was, "Who is this guy, and what's he all about?" I was trying to ask questions and find out what he was like, but nobody seemed to know much about him.

While Regier was trying to figure out what to do about Teddy as coach of the team, Dominik Hasek came out and said he didn't want to play for Teddy anymore. That was a case of Dom being Dom. Too many times Dom would just say something and not think about what he was saying. There would be repercussions, and then he'd backpedal. Dom was an intelligent guy, but he got himself in a lot of trouble with some of the things he said.

Everything that went on with Dom in the Ottawa series the previous spring, and all of the other stuff, made the team that much more special. The guys dealt with Dom's comments, and never let it affect the way they played. But Dom caused so many problems for the guys. He never realized that we had to deal with the repercussions too.

Eventually, Darcy offered Teddy a one-year contract. Teddy turned it down, and Darcy decided to hire someone else. I don't know if Darcy had any intention of signing Teddy to come back as coach. A new general manager usually brings in his own coach. I can understand that. Any GM is going to put his stamp on the team, and that's what happened.

Teddy deserved to be an NHL coach, and I was surprised that it took him so long to get another job. He was a motivator for us, a guy who people loved to play for. He wasn't an Xs and Os guy. Assistant coach Donny Lever had that role. Don was the brains behind that coaching staff. But everyone worked together.

That sort of approach has gotten very rare today. Too many times it's the coach's way or no way. Teddy was one of the few who would communicate with his players. "What's wrong? What do we need to do?" he'd ask. Then he and Donny would go figure out how to solve it.

After a search, Darcy settled on Lindy Ruff as the new coach. Lindy was in Buffalo during my first training camp in 1988. He was traded to the New York Rangers during that season, so when I was with the Sabres, I lived in Lindy's house with Grant Ledyard and his wife. At least I had a connection. When Ruff got the job, he wanted to know what was going on, and I talked to him about it. He was good that way. He was open-minded. He came in and said, "There's something good here. I'm just going to come in and pick up where they left off." And that's pretty much what he did. Lindy knew he had the basis of a team, and he tried to improve on it.

Pat LaFontaine's situation was messed up going into that training camp. He thought he had recovered from his concussion and would be ready for training camp, but the Sabres said doctors weren't so sure. So Patty worked out on his own. It didn't affect the team that much. It was only one player, and we knew Patty would be there when he was ready to go. He was intelligent enough to do what he had to do to be sure he was OK. He wasn't going to do anything crazy or off the wall. We just had to go play and hope we got him back. We never did, as Patty was eventually traded to the Rangers.

Outside of Patty, we didn't make too many changes that off-season. Garry Galley left as a free agent, and we picked up Jason Woolley to replace him. Wools fit in great. He was a great team guy. Lindy had him as an assistant coach in Florida, so he already knew what type of character he was. They didn't want to disrupt the chemistry of the team, so they were very careful about whom they brought in.

As the 1997-98 season was about to start, the front office became nervous about the sort of reception Dom would get from the home fans on opening night. It turned out he got a mix of cheers and boos. Dom had an on-again, off-again relationship with the fans. One day they loved him, the next day they hated him. They weren't really sure how to feel. And he was the type of guy that was so fragile that if they did boo him, it would bother him. Dom was a different bird. Most of the time you stood back, let him do his own thing, and made sure he didn't do anything stupid along the way. But he made up for his off-ice antics with his on-ice performance.

We had our typical slow start that season, in part because Alexei Zhitnik and Michael Peca were unsigned. So we just tried to hold it together until everyone was there. It's funny how the attitudes toward guys not signing their contracts by the start of regular season changed from when I first came into the league. At the beginning of my career, the guys thought it was selfish to do that—"Are you putting yourself in front of the team?" But when the years went by and hockey became more of a business, guys were sitting back saying, "That could be me. It might be me next year. So let's support the guy and let him do what he's got to do." Instead of one guy a year, there were three or four every year holding out. Eventually they signed, and we picked it up.

Dom got it going, and we were learning to play well in front of him. Dom had five shutouts for the month of December, and there were a lot of nights when we only gave up about 20 shots. The Sabres became a very good defensive team. In fact, some nights Dom was doing crazy things to keep his head in the game because he wasn't seeing many shots.

Lindy stresses a good defensive game plan. If you limit the other team's shots, you limit their scoring opportunities. Mike Ramsey was the defensive coach, and Rammer brought in a style that featured blocking shots—a simple game but an effective game. He taught guys to clear the front of the net, get the puck out of the zone—little things. Rammer was never a flashy player, but he was effective. He taught that style to the younger defensemen, and they were effective doing that.

Dom kept going into 1998 and right up through the Olympics in Nagano, Japan. That was the first time that the NHL players had been allowed in the Games, and Dom was the star. He led the Czech Republic to the gold medal, and he became a national hero by the time the Olympics were over. Richard Smehlik was on the Czech team too.

When they came back to the NHL and Buffalo after winning the gold, there was activity around those guys everywhere we went. The politicians in every major city we visited would throw parties for them. There would be events the nights before games. These guys were living a rock-star life while they were playing, although we still needed them to help us win. The attention level for our team went from 5 to 8 overnight, on a scale of 1 to 10. People wanted to see Dom play after the Olympics.

When the Olympic commotion died down, it was back to business. As we got close to the trading deadline, some of the talk was about Barnaby. I remember there was a night in Tampa when Lindy wasn't playing Matthew, so he sat at the end of the bench and put a white towel on the end of his stick and started waving it around. Typical Matthew. Some guys took it to heart, and some guys didn't really care. A day or so later, we had a meeting in the dressing room with the coaches. There was a flare-up between Matthew and Lindy. Many thought Matthew would be traded, but he wound up staying on the team.

Fans might think such confrontations are unusual, but they happen all the time. There are often fights between guys in the dressing room between periods. When people spend so much time together and play in such high-pressure circumstances, someone is bound to crack once in a while. The key point is that everyone has to understand that when it's over, it's over. Barney and Lindy said their piece, and they walked away from it. If you start holding a grudge every time somebody says something, you're going to be a bitter man for a long time.

That was right about the time the Rigas family took over the ownership of the team from the original ownership group that included the Knoxes. The sale had been in the works for some time, but it was still sad to see it happen. The Knoxes made me feel like I was part of a family.

The Knoxes didn't really run the Sabres like a business. They were content to lose a little money or break even, but they wanted everyone happy. They wouldn't get rid of a player unless something happened that forced them to agree to a trade. Now hockey is much more of a business, and the owners are businessmen. But the Sabres got lucky again, because Tom Golisano is a fan of the game, just like Seymour and Norty were. I think that's good for hockey.

The switch in ownership from the Knoxes to the Rigases really didn't have any effect on the players, because we didn't deal with those guys. They were busy running the organization. The players deal with the general manager and the coaching staff, and once in a while with the scouting staff.

We finished sixth in the conference that year. We didn't score many goals, but we had the goaltending to win a lot of one-goal games. We sure didn't win many blowouts.

The Philadelphia Flyers were our first-round opponent in 1998. The Sabres had lost to the Flyers a lot in the playoffs over the years, but we didn't feel like there was a jinx or anything. Too many times, even now, teams use the Flyers and Toronto as measuring sticks, especially in the Eastern Conference. They are supposed to be the big guns. The Flyers were always made out to be better than what they were, because they lived on reputation. But our teams in the late 1990s always found success against them. There were years when the Flyers did not want to play us because they knew we could beat them. They were big but a little slow, and we were fast and gritty enough to stand up to them, and we had great goaltending. In addition, the Flyers depended on two lines back then, and we had four lines that we rolled all the time. It made a big difference.

The Sabres won the series in five games, and Michal Grosek scored the overtime goal in Game Five to wrap it up. That might have been Michal's best moment as a Sabre. He was traded to Chicago a couple of years later in the Doug Gilmour trade and bounced around a bit after that. He never got the opportunity that he got in Buffalo. Michal has a unique personality; you have to understand him and know how to deal with him. When he was a Sabre, he was young and he got handled differently than he would have in other places. Other teams might have expected him to come and play like he did in Buffalo, but maybe there was a reason why he played the way he did here. Michal's confidence always needed a boost—push him and show him what to do, and he can go do it.

That's not uncommon. If you look at a professional athlete in our business—not in football, because I've never met a player who wasn't confident—his confidence is low. A lot of guys can't handle everything that's going on. I've never been around people that were so insecure all the time. Everyone is worried about his job. They're worried about how they are playing. They're worried about what other people are thinking. What does the coach think? What do the fans think? Considering how good they are at what they do, it was sick to see guys be so insecure about everything else.

Once we won the first round, we looked around and saw the top three seeds (New Jersey, Pittsburgh, and Philadelphia) had been eliminated. Washington, Montreal, Ottawa, and the Sabres were left. We didn't think about anything except the next round. Nobody on the team had ever been to the Conference Finals, so we just took it one round, one game at a time. We were having fun as we went along. Every day was a learning experience. Guys just fed off the excitement around the town, and the further we went, the better it was.

We played the Canadiens in the second round, and most people remember Game Two in Buffalo. Barnaby scored a hat trick on Mother's Day with his mother in the stands.

You could ask him right now, and he'd say it was the greatest day in his hockey career. Matthew finally got an opportunity to perform in the playoffs, and he stepped up. He wanted to play, and he could handle the responsibility. That game was the springboard for us winning that series. Guys fed off that so much. We said, "We can beat those guys," and we ended up sweeping the Canadiens.

When Brad May scored in overtime to beat the Bruins in 1993, it was like we had won the Stanley Cup in Buffalo. It was the first time we had won a playoff series in ten years. Now we were going to the conference finals for the first time since 1980. It was almost as if the Sabres had come out of the depths of the earth to become a respected team again. We were getting more attention around the league. People were saying in Buffalo, "Maybe there is something here now."

The next round was against Washington, with all their big guns—Peter Bondra, Olaf Kolzig, those types of guys. It was easy to wonder, how can we beat these guys? That's when we started to think about winning the Stanley Cup. It was only two series—eight wins—away. At this point of the playoffs, I wasn't playing much, but I accepted it. I didn't complain. The playoffs have a different style. The approach changes from team to team as you move along. I think by that time, we had guys in and out of the lineup all year, so it really didn't matter. I remembered that I could be put in the lineup at any time. I just kept myself in shape, ready to go. I wanted to play, but being part of it was just as good.

In the Conference Finals, no one knows what's going to happen. You'd like to say you can control what's going to happen, but you really can't. In this case, the Capitals were a more mature team, and I think they handled the commotion of playing in the Conference Finals a little better than we did. Perhaps that's the biggest reason why we lost in six games.

I guess we were at the point where we were happy to be there: "The Conference Finals—this is cool." The Capitals wanted it a little more than we did. Maybe they understood it a little more. I think we were young and didn't know what it took to get to the next level.

The one surprise of that series was that Dom let in some bad goals at key times. You never expected him to let in the weak goal.

We became so dependent on him that we took him for granted. We just thought he'd be there all the time. Then he had a bad night, and all the blame was on him.

Still it had been a great run, and it gave us a lot of confidence. The guys realized what it took to advance in the playoffs, and we knew we could play with the big guys. Going into the next season, that was a major help.

11

FINALLY

We felt pretty good about the team we had after the 1997-98 season, and General Manager Darcy Regier didn't have to make many changes. But we did lose one player in the expansion draft. The Nashville Predators had a choice between Bob Boughner and Dixon Ward, and they picked Bob. When we lost Bob, we lost a big part of the team in terms of chemistry. Bob was a gritty guy and a great team guy. He played a role for us that we missed.

The Sabres surprised some people in the summer of 1998 by going after a couple of the top free agents. They talked to Doug Gilmour and Ron Francis, two Hall of Famers, but couldn't sign either of them. Either of them would have helped us. Gilmour went to Chicago, and Francis signed with Carolina. Darcy did bring in James Patrick as a spare defenseman that summer, and that was a good move because he replaced Boughner on the roster. We all thought Patrick would be here for one year, but he was still around in 2004. James is a super guy, and everyone knew then he'd be a coach someday. He filled that role while he was playing; he was almost like a coach on the ice.

We went to Austria for a couple of exhibition games that season and then came back for an uneventful regular season in some ways. We had a solid first half, but there was a problem: Donald Audette's contract situation. Donald had been holding out all season, and he was traded to Los Angeles for a second-round draft choice in December—no player or players, just a draft choice. I wished that we could have gotten someone who could have helped us right away, but I obviously don't know what sort of offers we received for Donald.

In February Dom pulled a groin muscle, which started a story that would drag on for more than a year. Every time Dom got hurt, we went back to the Ottawa series in 1997. There was always a question floating in the background. People would ask, "Is he faking?" We had to deal with that whole mess again. He missed about a month. When he came back, Dom dictated when he could play and what he wanted to do, which was fine—as long as he played and played well.

Darcy was busy around the trading deadline in March. He sent Matthew Barnaby to Dallas for Stu Barnes in a deal that really helped us. Stewie is a great leader because he leads by example. He's not a real vocal guy, but he's great defensively and he can chip in on offense too. Matthew, on the other hand, can get under your skin but stay under control. There are few guys who can play the type of game Barnaby did, so we had to get quality in return for somebody like him.

We also traded Mike Wilson to Florida for Rhett Warrener. Getting a guy like Rhett, a young guy who played a physical role and fit into the chemistry, was great. Lindy had him in Florida, so he knew what he was getting. Rhett added a dimension of toughness. He had been to the finals before, ande were weak on experience, so it helped to have a guy like that around for the playoffs—a defensive defenseman with that edge in his play.

We also traded Derek Plante for a draft choice and got Joe Juneau right at the deadline. Nothing against Joe, but that was something of a letdown. Everyone thought we might need a little more offense to take the next step in the playoffs.

We finished in seventh place and felt pretty good going into the postseason. We had gained a lot of confidence that we could play with the big guys, and the additions made everyone even more comfortable. We also knew it didn't matter where we finished in the conference. Once you get to the playoffs, it's a totally different game. Everybody has a shot at the Cup. Look at Calgary in 2004. The Flames killed themselves to get into the playoffs, and they made it all the way to the finals. In this day and age, sometimes it hurts a team to be a top seed because of the work it takes just to get there. Then when the playoffs start, the team has nothing left.

The playoffs are a completely different experience from the regular season when it comes to preparation. The difference, of course, is that you play the team in the playoffs as many as seven straight times.

Before a regular-season game, the coaches may show the players a little videotape on the other team's power play, a little tape on their penalty kill, and that's it. They may talk about certain individuals. But when it comes to the playoffs, the coaches hand out pamphlets and books on the other team. They spend a ton of time breaking down the other team's power play. Every tendency of a guy comes up. It's totally unbelievable, especially with all the video equipment. There's nothing that gets away. Most guys do the same things all the time or close to it, so the players know everything about every player on the other team. There are no surprises.

We didn't play well in the first playoff game against Ottawa, getting outshot, 41–15, but we still won, 2–1. Dom was amazing. I talked to some of the guys from Ottawa about that game a few years later, and they told me that after the first game they were done. They knew in their heads that there was no possible way that they were going to beat us. They were mentally screwed right off the hop, and we beat them four straight.

That first win really got them off their game; they started to play our style instead of their own. We were hitting, using our good speed, playing physical hockey, and finishing our checks. As soon as they started trying to do that, they totally got off their game and had to rely on skill alone.

After playing three rounds in the playoffs the previous year, we knew how to handle the situation a lot better. You've got to be relaxed during the postseason, especially after winning a series or two. Players who get too wired may lose a little bit of focus and a little bit of that edge. The further teams go in the playoffs, the more pressure builds up. So the coaches go to greater extremes to motivate the players.

The playoffs are mentally draining too. You're playing every other night, night after night, and it's increasingly intense. You've got to be able to turn the switch on and off. You can't be totally mentally dialed in for that seven-game series over two weeks or you'll be dead by the end of it. So you have to learn to be focused on that day. On the off-days, you have to be ready to wind down and then turn it on again. Playoff experience helps you learn how to do that.

Next up in the playoffs in '99 was Boston. The Bruins had a different style from Ottawa—they weren't as fast, but they were a little more rugged and had a little more experience. We opened in Boston and didn't really know what to expect at first. They had some experienced players, but we worked a little better as a team.

We split the first two games in Boston and then won all our home games to take it in six games. Our "checking" line was getting a lot of attention around that time. Michael Peca, Dixon Ward, and Vaclav Varada did a great job on Alexei Yashin's line in the Ottawa series, and they followed it up against Jason Allison's line against Boston.

Those guys were so good defensively. Pecs dominated the face-offs. Dixon was phenomenal along the boards and in the corner. Vaclav caused havoc out there—everybody was more worried about what he was doing than what they were doing. He allowed the others to work together. Pecs and Dixon were good offensively too. They had an awful lot of room when V was running around, playing his game. Those guys played all the time too. You can call them a "third line," but they were the clutch line.

It's kind of unusual for one line to stick together for any length of time these days, but that line sure did. They jelled when they got put together. In the regular season, you often play with different guys. Coaches will change the lines during the game when things aren't working well, looking for something. And something that works today might not work tomorrow. What didn't work yesterday might work today. Coaches have to keep throwing lines out there to see what works. But Pecs' line always seemed to work.

The emotion of the playoffs jumped to a whole new level when we found out we were going to play the Toronto Maple Leafs in the Eastern Conference finals. The guys always want to play against Toronto, regular season or the playoffs. It's so much better now that they are in the Eastern Conference. Years ago they were stuck in the West and we'd play them once or twice a year. It was smart to put them back in the East.

There are so many guys in the league from the Toronto area, and anybody who grew up in Canada watched *Hockey Night in Canada*. Back then, Toronto and Montreal played on TV all the time. I can still remember being excited in my first few years in the NHL when I was going to be on *Hockey Night*, because everyone back home could watch me play.

While we had some great games with Toronto in the regular season, rivalries really get going during the playoffs. And it doesn't matter what kind of team Toronto has, the Leafs always make themselves out to be the hockey gods. Their opponents would shake their heads and turn up their intensity. I think that's why Toronto has some trouble at times. Everybody wants to stick it to the Leafs and works extra hard to do so.

It was our second straight year in the conference finals, of course, and we were more confident this time. We knew what it was going to be like—the attention that the series attracted was unbelievable. We had guys on our team say that it was a letdown to get to the finals.

The first game against the Leafs in Toronto was pretty dramatic. Dom had a sore groin, but no one knew about it until right before the game. Dwayne Roloson came in for Dom. In a way Dom's absence was good for us. Guys were thinking before the start of the game, "Oh, man, we have to worry about our own zone a little more." But Rollie had played well for us all year. It wasn't as if there was a confidence problem. We just pulled together a little tighter.

We beat the Leafs with Rollie in goalie in the first game, and that's what we wanted to do. Obviously, when you're on the road at the start of a series, you want to win one of the first two. In fact, we almost beat them again in the second game, again with Rollie in goal. After that we knew we had a good chance of winning, so coming back to Buffalo we felt very comfortable. The Leafs must have been thinking at that point, "It's not going to happen."

We won Games Three and Four in Buffalo with Dom back. By that time I think the Leafs felt their only chance was if Rollie stayed in goal, so Dom's return was another confidence booster for us. We played really well at home. Knowing how big that fourth game was—they would either be right back in the series or we'd have them by the throats—we played well for the whole game. We never had a letdown.

What's more, I got the game-winning goal in Game Four. I've still got the stick from that one. Barnes passed it out from the side wall. I had my back to the net. The puck was in the air, and I just tried to knock it down and then turn and fire. I knocked it down so hard it went between my legs and between Curtis Joseph's legs into the net. It caught us both off guard.

Game Four was pretty much it. After that, it was just a matter of driving to Toronto for the next game. It's funny how you can tell when a team is beaten in the playoffs. Teams act differently when they are coming on and off the ice. Their heads are down all the time, and they aren't as spirited on the ice, and they aren't trying to do that little extra. There were only a few guys on the Leafs who still believed they could win. It's a whole different look than you get in the regular season when guys just say "Who cares?" and get the game over so that they can get on the plane and go to the next city. In the playoffs, you can even tell when a team is beaten by how the players do interviews, and how they act around the rink or in practice.

We won Game Five, wrapping it up with an empty-netter by Dixon. Many people remember more about what happened after the game than during it. The Wales trophy came out for winning the conference championship, and nobody touched it in the ceremony. Peca, our captain, wouldn't go near it.

The subject had come up before the game—"If we win, we don't touch it [the trophy]. It's unlucky." I thought, "Let's see this thing." To this day, I've never seen that trophy except for the little replica I've got in my trophy case. Dave Andreychuk did the same thing as Peca did when the Lightning won the conference championship in 2004.

I don't really understand that sort of thinking. If you are that superstitious, try something else. We worked hard to get that trophy; wouldn't it have been nice to get a picture with it if only to say, "Yeah, I won that thing"? But at that point, who cared? We weren't thinking about that part of it. We were thinking, "We're going to the finals."

One of the highlights of my career was the bus ride from Toronto back to Buffalo that night. It was something. Everyone was excited, talking on cell phones, going nuts for two hours. We all drank beer and had a good time.

We were feeling rowdy by the time we got to the border. The customs agent came on the bus and walked to the back. He had a serious look, but then he yelled something like "Leafs suck" or "Go Sabres." All of a sudden, Dom grabbed the man's head and poured a beer over the agent's head. We went from all fired up to stone quiet, as if to say, "Oh, oh, what did you just do, Dom?" But the guy loved it. He just went nuts, running down the aisle, high-fiving everybody, and then got off the bus. For one night, we were walking on top of the world.

We got home, and all the guys and their wives went out. The whole team came together that night. Everything was forgotten except for the fact that we were getting the opportunity to play for the Cup. It was pretty special.

Lindy and the rest of the coaching staff obviously were doing a great job in the playoffs. It's funny—I didn't think of Lindy as a future coach when I first met him. He was a jokester as a player, a fun guy, but he was obviously a fast learner when it came to coaching.

Looking back, it's amazing how fast the time went by at that point. Before we knew it we were getting ready to head down to Dallas. We didn't have much time to celebrate; we were right back at it. We secluded ourselves from everybody and concentrated on what we needed to do. It was a neat experience.

If you compared their roster to our roster, it was easy to think we were going to get killed in the series. They had all the stars. But everybody on both sides was nervous. There weren't many guys on either team that had been in the finals before. We didn't know what it was going to be like. We hadn't played in Dallas since the first game of the season way back in October, so the opening games provided a stage for both teams to feel each other out.

We won the first game in overtime when Jason Woolley scored. Once that was over, the whole idea that they were better because they had Brett Hull, Mike Modano, and Ed Belfour went out the window. We proved to ourselves that we could play with them. We also played well in the second game but lost, so we came home feeling pretty good.

The intensity on the ice in the finals is amazing. Both teams have their games so fine-tuned, and everyone is so afraid of making a mistake. Every time you're on the ice, you give it every drop you've got to try to make a difference. For most guys it's the biggest thing in their lives to get to that point. They grew up watching the finals. Every person wants to be the guy to make that difference. He wants to be the guy who people talk about. Each player does every little thing on the ice that he can to help his team win. It's not like the middle of the season, when guys just float through the game on some nights. The guys that play a lot of minutes in the finals have nothing left by the time the game is over.

In fact, playing four rounds in the postseason—two months—is an incredible grind. I could never have imagined what it was like until I experienced it. It could go on for 28 games, but they weren't like 28 games in the regular season. Teams play every other night. There's travel all the time. Bodies don't have time to recover. Everyone takes a beating because the intensity level is so much higher. You just don't have time for those bruises to come out. They just get deeper and deeper over time. Bad knees get worse.

Everyone plays hurt in the finals when they normally wouldn't. If there's something wrong with you in the regular season, you don't play. In the finals, you ice it down, freeze it, and go. It's not as if the coaches have to push you to get out there, either. Every player knows what he has to do at that point. You only get so many chances, so you do what you have to do to get there.

We came home for Game Three, and we sat back a little too much. I think we were a little nervous. I don't believe home-ice advantage in the playoffs means anything. Sometimes it's better to start out on the road, go and win a game, and then play at home. When you play at home, all the pressure is on the home team. It's your crowd and your media there. Plus, there are things you have to deal with away from the rink that can be distractions. You have people coming in for games, trying to get tickets set up. You have family staying at your house. When you're on the road, it's just hockey. You just go play.

I think after the third game, we realized we couldn't sit back, we couldn't be tentative, we couldn't be nervous. We had to play our game, and that's what we did to win Game Four. We were happy to come out of there, 2–2. It was a whole different story than if had been were down, 3–1.

Back in Dallas, we didn't play well in Game Five and lost. To make matters worse, Rhett broke his ankle right at the end of the game. That was a big loss. Rhett was the guy who cleared people from the net. On Hull's goal in Game Six, a guy like Rhett would have had him cleared out of there. All of a sudden Darryl Shannon had to go into the lineup, and he hadn't played since the first couple of games in the Ottawa series. I think some of the guys were saying to themselves, "Oh, no, Rhett's gone." They realized how big a part of it he was. But then everyone thought, "We've won without Dom. We've won without other people. So we can win without Rhett."

I don't think we played that badly in Game Six, but we couldn't get to the net. They played great defensively. That's what Ken Hitchcock, the Dallas coach at the time, is known for—good defense. Still, we were confident we could play with them, and we proved it.

We got some chances. Barnes tied the game in the third period, and we went into overtime. Once that happens, the game changes. Obviously we had to be careful because we didn't want to give up any scoring chances, but we couldn't sit back and let the Stars come to us. Sometimes Lindy is more selective on who goes out on the ice after regulation, and everyone holds his breath on every shot because anything can happen. It never seems like a nice goal is scored in overtime; it's always an ugly goal.

And the intensity level that's already high during the game goes even higher in overtime. Guys work even harder. Any little mistake can cost your team the game, and you don't want to be the person who makes it. Guys squeeze the stick a little tighter and make sure they make the right play.

Game Six went on and on, and as a scratch I watched most of the overtimes from the dressing room, although I was out in the tunnel at times, too—back and forth. I couldn't stay still.

Everyone watching remembers how it ended, as Hull scored the game-winning goal with his foot in the crease. OK, it happened. The officials' view was that it was a goal. But according to the rules, it was not a goal.

I was with some of the other guys who weren't playing that night. We saw the replay in the dressing room, and so we came out and yelled that Hull's foot was in the crease. By that time, Lindy was trying to argue with the ref. But 30 seconds after the goal went in, there were a hundred people on the ice. The Cup was there in a minute or two. And because it was so late—1:45 in the morning—I think they were trying to get it wrapped up and over with. We never had an opportunity to argue. It was called, the game was over, and we were told not to be such sore losers. But the league officials knew that it shouldn't have counted after looking at it; anybody would have known.

By the time the replay officials realized what was going on and could have said, "What are you doing?" everyone who could have changed the ruling was gone. They just disappeared, probably because it was so late. That's the part that bothered me. Lindy yelled at NHL Commissioner Gary Bettman, who gave him a look that said, "Shut up and get in the dressing room." We were dumbfounded. Nobody on our team knew what to do. Nobody paid any attention to what we had to say. What were they going to do, take all of those people off the ice and resume play? We knew we were done.

It's funny that a goal like that decided the Cup. There had been arguments about the discretionary rule all year, which made it all the more terrible to lose that way. If it had been a normal goal, well, so be it. We all look back at it, and people still talk about it. We should have had another chance.

The NHL never admitted it made a mistake. If they had known how much it meant to so many people, someone would have checked the play more closely. Who cared if it was five in the morning? Check it. It wasn't Game Three. We didn't have any nights left to redeem ourselves. The players on that team still just shake their heads thinking about it—it could have been us. We could possibly have won the Stanley Cup. I'm not saying we would have won—who knows? But to lose the right way would have been much easier to stomach.

A couple of days later, the city had a rally for us downtown, and that was pretty cool. In fact, it was a total surprise. We just knew we had to go to the rink that day, but when we got together, we were told we were going to the rally. At first everyone thought, "This is kind of stupid. I want to go home. I want to see my family." But it was neat to see the fans in Niagara Square and see the support involved. Guys still talk about that.

That rally showed that Buffalo is a town that respects what it has. People say that it doesn't matter if you win or lose as long as you show up and play hard, and I think the fans were showing those feelings. Sure everybody would have liked a championship, but they respected us for leaving everything we had out there—just like they did the Bills in football during all of their losing Super Bowl years.

Lindy ended the rally by saying, "No goal." It was a time to say his piece. I think everybody understood what had happened. But they knew there was nothing we could do, and after a few months the anguish died away. The emotion only comes back at certain times.

It was great to play for the Stanley Cup, but the way it ended spoiled the feeling a bit. Even today it's tough to talk about it, because we came *that close*.

12

END OF AN ERA

It doesn't take long to realize that one season is over, and the next one is coming soon. One of the Dallas Stars found that out right after winning the Stanley Cup in 1999. I remember how on the day that the Stars were having their Cup celebration party in Dallas, Roman Turek was told in the middle of the festivities that he wouldn't be with the team any longer. He was exposed and had been taken in the expansion draft. See you later, thanks a lot—that's the way the business can be, and it stinks.

We were feeling lucky the year before (1998), when we made it to the Conference Finals, and the next year we made it to the final. But to get through to a championship ... well, the odds were against us. With the right changes, maybe it could happen. But we knew it would be difficult.

In fact, the roster changed a lot once again by the end of the 1999-2000 season, and the team was never the same. That 1999 team we had was special, but we weren't able to capitalize on it again. It's not every day you can put a team like that together. It takes time.

And we sure didn't have a lot of time during the off-season that summer. By the time we got done with the finals, it was June 19.

Players usually start working out for the upcoming season around June 1. If we took a month off to rest from the end of the playoffs, it would almost have been the first of August—four weeks before we had to be at camp.

And this was our second straight year of having a short off-season, because we had played until June 4 in 1998. It's tough when teams go that far, back to back. There was excitement in 1999 from playing in the finals, but at some point that summer, everyone just went "blaaaaahhhh." We were dead physically. It took a month or so just before we could start lifting our shoulders again. Players need a month off before they can train again, but we didn't have that luxury.

That's why it's stupid for the season to go as long as it does. The NHL should shorten the season or at least trim the playoffs a little bit. It would help everyone in the league. Hockey is not like baseball, where you can play every day. In football, they play once and take a week off before they play again. And those guys play a few seconds at a time for half the game. There aren't many sports like hockey, with the travel involved and the pounding that's taken. But there's a lot of money involved, and the owners don't want to compensate the players unless they think they are getting their money's worth.

The summer of 1999 was pretty quiet, with one big exception for me. I received the King Clancy Award from the National Hockey League for community work. Kenny Martin of the Sabres community relations department helped me win that. I was never going to win an individual trophy because of the way I played. That was the one I could win. I have the trophy for winning the conference championship, the Presidents' Cup (best regular-season record in the league for when I was in Ottawa), and the King Clancy

Trophy. That's three trophies, and I'm very proud of that.

It makes me feel good to help out charities when I can. One of the first things I ever did in that area was to work with the March of Dimes golf tournament. The organizers were looking for an honorary chairman of sorts, and my mom worked with the March of Dimes, so it was a natural connection. I did that tournament for 13 years.

When I was playing with the Sabres, we used to go to Children's Hospital and Roswell Park in Buffalo a great deal. We'd see kids, and that put a smile on their faces. I tried to make them feel a little special. It took their minds away from what they were going through, even if only for a few minutes. And on occasion I had a parent come up to me and say, "It's the first time I've seen my kid smile in months," which made us both feel good. I've had people come up to me out of the blue and say, "Remember me?" A lot of times I don't, but then they'll say, "You came up to see me at Children's when I was sick ten years ago, but I'm doing good now," and that puts a smile on my face too. Some of the kids aren't so lucky, of course, but it's nice to know I could help some of them feel better for a little while at least.

I heard that I'd won the Clancy trophy a week in advance, which gave me time to make preparations. It is the only one of the major NHL awards for which the winner is known in advance; three finalists are announced for the others, and the winners are announced on a television show in Toronto.

I took my mom, dad, and sister to the ceremony, and they were proud to be there. I got to publicly thank them for everything they did while I was up there on the podium with all the great players such as Wayne Gretzky and Mario Lemieux. Sometimes players of that caliber would roll their eyes when players like me were on the ice, but on the stage that night, we were equal. I was one of them.

**

We paid the price for those last two playoff runs with a bad start the next season. Then Dominik tore his groin muscle and missed the next several weeks of play. There wasn't too much panic when he got hurt, even though it was a big loss. We had learned to play well defensively, and the shots-against statistic had come down. There were nights when he faced fewer than 20 shots. When a goalie sees so few shots, his team has a very good chance of winning. But the whole team has to play well defensively for that to happen.

One of the odd moments of the season for me came on November 30, when Matthew Barnaby came back to Buffalo with the Pittsburgh Penguins.

Yes, Matthew and I had a fight. He was just playing his game, ticking everyone off. It was one of those times when he had to go do something. I can remember grabbing on to him and saying, "Would you just shut up? Just shut up!" That fight didn't have to happen. I didn't want to do it—"Just play the game, and get it over with," I thought. So we fought, and I knocked two of his teeth out. We laughed about it afterward, but his wife gave it to both of us after the game. I think I fought him three times in all after he was traded. But that time was the only time I was mad at him. The other times, I did it just to do it.

We stumbled along for most of that season. I think we were feeling the pressure of trying to match the previous two years. It's not like guys weren't trying, but little was working. We were used to the wins coming pretty easily and naturally. And then when it didn't happen that way, we said, "OK, what do we do?" It wasn't as if our team had fallen completely apart, but we wondered what we had to do to get out of that funk.

General manager Darcy Regier made some moves that showed he hadn't given up on the season. He sent Michal Grosek to Chicago for Doug Gilmour and J.P. Dumont. Dougie instantly became one of the team leaders. With the exception of Dom, we hadn't had a player of that stature on the team for a long time, and he made his presence on the team known. Dougie was a guy that we had all watched while we were growing up, and everybody liked him. It was pretty nice for a guy to be at that level as a player and still be one of the boys. He was a breath of fresh air. The "other guy" in the deal ended up helping too. J.P. turned himself into a pretty good player. We saw that he had talent; he just needed some time.

Regier also acquired Chris Gratton from Tampa Bay. The new guys gave us just enough of a boost to get into the playoffs, even though we finished a game under .500. We tied Washington on the last day to clinch the playoff spot. Getting there was important, because it had been a difficult year.

Lindy Ruff received some criticism that year for putting too much pressure on individual players. I think that was true, but he was trying to get a little more out of the guys. By that point, the young team wasn't young anymore. We had experience. Guys had to be pushed to get to the next level. The pressure was on Lindy, so in turn he put it on the players.

But Lindy also understood whom he could push and whom he couldn't. By that time, he had gotten to know the guys. It was his third year, and he talked a lot about he knew it would take if we were going to be an upper-echelon team—we had to act like it, play like it, and be consistent like it.

But not too much worked perfectly that season. We met the

Flyers in the first round of the playoffs. Everyone remembers John LeClair's goal in the second game of that series. He took a shot that went through the webbing of the side of the net, but it was ruled a goal. That took the wind out of our sails. It was almost like we expected it, because our year had seemingly been filled with misfortune. Everyone muttered, "Here we go again." Doug had the flu and couldn't do much. Jay McKee missed most of the series with a bad shoulder, and Alexei Zhitnik was suspended for the deciding game. We were done in five games.

Right after the series, Dom and Dougie both said they would return for one more season in Buffalo. That sure made it like seem like the 2000-01 team was going to be our last good shot at the Cup. Then we brought in Dave Andreychuk as a free agent, and the feeling grew. When he and Doug came in, everyone in the dressing room was like, "Wow. Finally." Both of those guys were so well respected around the league that the young guys even glowed when Doug or Andy talked to them personally.

Andy's signing was a huge surprise. I didn't think he'd ever come back. I knew he was a little bitter when he left Buffalo in 1993, when he was traded to Toronto for Grant Fuhr. This time, he was excited. He thought he would come in here and finish his career in Buffalo.

While Andreychuk's return made us all feel optimistic, we watched Michael Peca's developing contract battle nervously. We knew it was business. Michael thought he needed to get a certain contract. I think eventually it turned personal between the two sides. Once that happened, there was no giving in. That was unfortunate, because we lost a guy who would have been a very big part of the team.

We had plenty of talent in 2000-01, but we had trouble getting players in the right spots. We had a lot of guys with similar skills, and they all were demanding ice time. It's tough to keep everyone happy in that situation. The situation at forward got even more crowded at the trading deadline. We got Donald Audette back in a trade from Atlanta and picked up Steve Heinze from Columbus. Donald was having a great year in Atlanta, and we hoped he'd be hot going into the playoffs. He was coming to a place where he was comfortable. It might have been a perfect fit had it worked. He knew a lot of the guys, knew the city, and knew the team.

I don't think we used our experience to its best advantage that season. When we brought in Dougie and Andy, I thought that was the kind of leadership and experience we needed. It wasn't a great regular season, particularly at the start, but that was no big deal. We just wanted to get into the playoffs. That was the attitude. There was no sense of urgency, and in a way, that was bad for us. We were a little complacent. Maybe we didn't go the extra mile to get ready for the playoffs. But at least we finished strong and ended up in fifth place in the conference.

We met the Flyers again in the first round of the playoffs that year. Some of the attention before the series went to a guy who wasn't even going to play: Eric Lindros had suffered some concussions and was out for the season.

Lindros is an interesting story. He came into the league as a first overall draft choice with huge expectations. The pressure of the world was on him. He was supposed to take over for Wayne Gretzky as the league's top superstar. Well, that's difficult. You have to be a strong person to handle that. Eric did well and had a good career, but maybe he didn't play up to the level of the expectations of some people.

Eric's problems seemed to start when he came out of junior hockey and said he wouldn't play for the Quebec Nordiques. He went to the Flyers in a huge trade. He was a young kid who was getting direction from his family, so he couldn't be blamed for that. What did he know? He was 18 years old. And what did his family know about that situation? His mother and father had never been through anything like that either. When people say Lindros should have handled his situation differently, I reply that no kid at that age is good at making those types of decisions.

The jump out of junior hockey is tough for everyone, and that includes the stars like Lindros. When a player gets to the NHL, he's probably already been a star at some level—minor hockey, junior, college, wherever. Once he gets to the pros, he has to fill a role. I wasn't expected to score when I played in the NHL. If I scored, that was a bonus, but my role to play physical and fight when I had to. On the other hand, goal-scorers are not expected to hit or fight or block shots. Sometimes, a player has to change his role to an entirely different style to fit in with a new team, and that's not easy.

Lindros never played another game with the Flyers, and they could have used him in the playoffs. We won three of the first five games and had the chance to wrap things up at home in Game Six. That's the one everyone remembers from that series because we won the game by 8–0.

It's pretty amazing that a team can be so mentally unprepared to make a game out of it in that situation, but from the beginning, that was not a contest. We got a couple of goals early, and it was over. I've been in those games on both sides, and losing them is a terrible feeling. You just want to get it over with. Everything seems to go wrong. The harder you work, the less goes right. That happens during the regular season too. Sometimes your goaltending struggles or you can't score or defensively you're slack. The person who arrives at the answer as to why that happens will be rich.

That game and series gave us a lot of confidence. Philadelphia was always bigger and stronger than we were and had more star players. We played them well, just like we did against Toronto and New Jersey. We could handle those guys; we just never got to play them enough in the playoffs. We'd usually get stuck with someone we'd struggle against, and it was never when we were at our best.

The Pittsburgh Penguins were next, and they were one of those teams we struggled to beat. They had Mario Lemieux, Jaromir Jagr, Alexei Kovalev, and Martin Straka. Our problem was that we always tried to play the Penguins' game—wide-open, wheel-and-deal garbage. That wasn't our style. We only had two or three guys who could play that way. The rest of the guys couldn't, or shouldn't. It killed us. I can't remember a time when we went in there and whipped them or beat them up. We never could.

Mario was just back from retirement at that point, but he was still great. He was a big guy who could move well—he reminded me of the Flyers' Tim Kerr in that way. Mario's agility was great. Usually guys that big can't handle the puck as well, especially in tight quarters. But Mario was different. And the thing I liked about him was he didn't hesitate to dish out a check. He played ticked off. He yelled and screamed at times, and he played with emotion. I remember he hit defenseman Jay McKee really hard one night. Oh my God, he almost killed him.

That was a funny series. The Penguins won the first two games in Buffalo, and then we won the next three games to take the lead. We came close to winning that series in Game Six in Pittsburgh. We led by a goal with less than 90 seconds left. Then a shot from the point got deflected and went straight up in the air. Mario spun around, slapped it, and got it past Dom. Yes, there was still overtime, but that deflated us for the rest of the night. It was a freak goal. Nobody had made a mistake. Everyone was covered. Mario was just so big and lanky that he was able to get a stick on it.

Alexei Kovalev scored in overtime to set up a Game Seven. We weren't as down going into that game as some people think. It would have been different if they had scored with 80 seconds left and won the series, because we would have had no chance to recover, but Game Six had nothing to do with the next game. Everybody in the media kept bringing up Mario's goal because we were so close. But we knew once the next game started, it would be forgotten. We couldn't sit and pout about it until then.

We played pretty well in Game Seven, but Robert Lang tied the game for the Penguins in the third period to send it to overtime. Every Sabre fan can picture the overtime goal. Darius Kasparaitis came in as a trailer on a rush, and he one-timed a shot past Hasek to win it.

I knew instantly that this was it for this group of guys, most of whom had come so close in 1999. Any Canadian kid dreams of winning the Stanley Cup. Nothing else—not making money or playing in an all-star game. You win it any way you can. We let it slip away once, and that hurt. After that we thought, "Are we ever going to get back there?" We thought we might, but sometimes things are out of your control.

Playoff eliminations are always a shock. It doesn't matter if it is Game Seven or Game Four. When the final buzzer goes and you are done for the year, the guys in the dressing room will never play together again. Some will be traded; others will go into contract battles; and a few will lose their jobs. You never know what will happen before the start of the next season. Everything is up in the air.

And if you are one of the guys thinking you might never play again, that's when getting knocked out of the playoffs is really awful.

A young kid can dream about next year, but once you get older, you don't know if there's a next year. You never do. That part is really terrible.

I was in that situation for a few years, which made losing much more difficult. I sat there when the buzzer went off, and said, "Is that it? What am I going to do now?"

13

TIME'S UP

The Buffalo Sabres were set to be a very different team in the fall of 2001 than they had been the previous spring. We traded two of our best players and lost a few other good ones to free agency.

Michael Peca's stay in Buffalo ended right after the Entry Draft, as he was traded to the New York Islanders for Tim Connolly and Taylor Pyatt. Then Dominik Hasek got his wish and was traded to Detroit for Slava Kozlov and a first-round draft pick. It wasn't enough for him to simply ask for a trade. He demanded his own destination, and then he said to Detroit, "Don't give up too much. I don't want to go if you give up too much." That's the way he was. That was the selfish side in him.

A year later, he said if he went into the Hall of Fame he'd go in as a Red Wing. You can imagine how well that went over. He was nothing when he came to Buffalo, where he finally got a chance to play regularly in the NHL. We gave him a lot of individual success. Never did he say, "Thanks, guys." It was always, "You never would have been here without me." That's garbage. We went from giving up 40 and 50 shots to fewer than 20 some nights. That's sound defensive hockey. It was pretty easy for him to look good in those games. Dom burned a few bridges with all that.

Then, Kozlov was grumpy right from the time he got to Buffalo. He didn't want to be here. That can't be blamed on anybody, but it didn't help. In the big picture, we'd traded Dom for a guy who could have helped us but didn't want to play for us ... and who wasn't shy about letting everyone know about it.

In addition to Hasek and Peca, we lost Doug Gilmour, Dave Andreychuk, Donald Audette, and Steve Heinze to free agency. That represented some big holes to fill, and there are always other changes on the team from year to year.

The first day of training camp that season was September 11, 2001. I remember being on the treadmill that morning. There were always televisions turned on in the workout area, dressing room, and player lounge, and the news was playing. When the networks reported the first plane hit the tower, everyone thought it was a mistake or something. Then the second plane hit, and everything stopped. We felt the way everyone felt—shocked and horrified.

We were in New York for a game two weeks later, and a bunch of us went down to Ground Zero. Everything there was covered in dust, and all the people were quiet. It was a unique experience.

It was interesting to hear from some of the other guys on the team in that situation. Some of the Europeans shared experiences with us, telling us stories about things that had happened at home of a similar nature. Stuff like that happens over there too, although obviously not to the scale of 9/11.

While we dealt with disaster, it became clear we needed a new captain with Peca gone, and we found one in Stu Barnes. That was a great move. He was a great guy who worked his butt off all the time. Stu said the right things, did the right things, and earned the respect of everyone in the room. We all were happy about his appointment.

Rhett Warrener and I were picked as the assistant captains, and we were there to supply the "rah-rah." Stu provided the sense of reason. It was a perfect situation.

Too many times the top-paid player on the team is picked to be the captain, which is wrong. He's not always the right guy. Just because someone has a captain's letter on his sweater doesn't mean guys are going to listen him. If they don't respect him, his title means nothing. That's the part of picking captains and assistants that bothers me sometimes. But this worked out well. Stu was one of our better players, but he worked hard on and off the ice. He communicated well. He never had an ego of any type. Everything was always well thought out, and nothing was off the cuff.

Meanwhile, I was proud to be an assistant captain. That was one of the best things to ever happen to me in hockey. I knew I'd never be a captain, and assistant captain was as far as I ever was going to get. One time I was asked to give it up to another player to make him feel a part of the team, and I said no. If I had done that, in my mind it would've taken away the reasoning behind the choice of an assistant captain. If it is given away to make someone play better, that player's not strong enough to deserve it. So I said no, and the issue was dropped.

When I was out there with a letter on my shirt, the referee and linesmen were apt to communicate with me a little better. In this day and age, a referee often has an ego bigger than the building. He doesn't think he needs to talk to anyone. That's a big problem with the whole officiating system. The lines of communication between the players, referees, and coaches are often not open. When the officials don't talk to others, it pushes buttons that raise a level of anger and frustration, and that's when the problems begin. Better communication would prevent a lot of problems from starting.

One time Andy VanHellemond skated over to the benches before an afternoon game in Boston and told everyone that he had a plane to catch right after the game and wasn't in the mood to take any arguing. That was good. Everyone knew where they stood before the game started and the game went smoothly. Too many times players can't question anything because to do so would question the knowledge of the referee ... and he thinks he knows everything. That's not true.

That season had plenty of ups and downs. We'd win a few games, then lose a few games. We all knew it would take a long time to get back to our previous level. Developing a team takes time, and we knew we were in for the long haul at that point.

Still, it looked like we had a chance to make a run at one of the last playoff spots, but we needed some different faces in the form of trades. When the team isn't going well, the first thing people think about is some sort of deal. We all get impatient, thinking a trade or two would help the team win right away. The front office has to be more patient. But I think we were sitting and waiting for the inevitable for much of the season anyway. When nothing had happened by January, it was really too late—we were almost out of the playoff picture. We became discouraged.

We had some guys who would have been happy to go elsewhere. Players like Richard Smehlik and Jason Woolley weren't playing much by then because the coaching staff was going with young guys like Dmitri Kalinin and Brian Campbell. Fans might ask about a veteran who has been scratched or benched, "Is he done?" Players don't think that way. They know from past experience what someone can do, and they believe that when push comes to shove, those players will be able to play at that level again. The only person who knows when it's time to retire is the player himself.

By this point there were rumors that the team would go bankrupt or simply close down. I wondered, "Am I going to have a job? What's going to happen? Will the players be sold off to other teams?" We didn't have any idea what was happening, and it's pretty hard to concentrate when you don't know what your future is.

I was a free agent that summer, but I didn't want to leave. Buffalo was my place, and I wanted to stay. If the team folded, I could go somewhere else, but I wanted to stick it out to the bitter end. Fortunately, the NHL put the Sabres on a budget and kept the team in business. They were looking to run the team for as little money as possible, and I was a good fit. I had a following around town, and the league was banking on that following still coming to games. We didn't have the flashiest team in the world, but there we had a lot of guys who people respected.

The start of the 2002-03 season, then, was filled with questions about the team. We didn't know if someone would buy and move the team. Sometimes new ownership will come in and change the entire direction of a team. We tried to figure out what was going to happen and constantly asked questions.

We won our first two games of the season but soon sank under .500 for good. Then in mid-January, the Sabres declared bankruptcy. Buffalo was the second NHL team to do that in 2002-03; Ottawa was the first. That was a red flag that there was a problem involving the entire league and its finances. If one team does it, you can blame it on how it was operated. When two teams declare bankruptcy, maybe there really is something wrong with the economics of the game.

Thomas Golisano started negotiations to purchase the team at that point, but it didn't help us on the ice much. We were still stumbling along. By early March, we knew it would take an incredible run to make the playoffs. The Sabres tried and failed ... but I wasn't around to see it.

About a month or two before the trade deadline in 2003, I was asked if I'd be interested in going to another team in a deal. I knew physical players were often moved around the deadline. But it would have had to be the right set of circumstances to get me to leave the Sabres at that point in my career. I wasn't going to go to another team just to go somewhere else. I wanted to go to a Stanley Cup contender.

Also, I had to know about my future with the Sabres. I asked about coming back the following year, and I was told that the chances of returning were not very good. So I said to myself, "Do I stay here and play it out? They don't want me anyway. Or, do I go to another team and maybe try to win?" After some thought, I told them, "If you work it out, fine."

On March 9, we were in Tampa when Darcy Regier told me after the game that Ottawa was interested in trading for me. I knew John Muckler, who by then had become the Senators' general manager, and some of the other guys up there. I said OK.

Our plane was delayed that night in Tampa. We hung out in Ybor City for a couple of hours, and the boys had a few beers. By the time I got on the bus, the whole bus was chanting, "Go, Sens. Go." Lindy Ruff stood up and yelled back, "Keep it down; that's not official yet," or something to that effect. It was pretty cool. The next day, the two sides worked it out ... and I was off to Ottawa.

It was tough to leave Buffalo, but this couldn't have worked out better for me at that point in my life. My junior team was 45 minutes from Ottawa in Cornwall, where my sister and her family live. My parents were two hours away in Stirling. It was perfect. I definitely wouldn't have gone to places like Calgary or Los Angeles.

I talked to Muckler that morning when the deal was finished. I felt even more comfortable about going there after talking to him. I believed what he was doing with the Senators was the right way to go. He was trying to build a team that could make a run at a Cup. Mucks would do anything he could to win. A lot of guys don't have the guts to make moves.

When I got down to the arena for the trade announcement, Stu Barnes was there too. He had been traded to Dallas, and Stewie was devastated. The trade came out of the blue for him, and it was a major shock. I still don't completely understand that, since it was pretty obvious that the Sabres were going to be rebuilding and any of the veterans were liable to be going somewhere else. I was a little more prepared for it. We were sitting in the office of Rip Simonick, our equipment manager, and Stu started crying. I knew he was a wreck, and we were about to go in for a news conference.

"Don't worry about it," I told Stu. "I'll say whatever and try to deflect the attention from you."

The poor guy couldn't even talk. I joked around in the news conference to try to help him out.

Afterward, I jumped in the car and started driving to Ottawa. I was leaving my life behind, and I wondered when I was going to be back in Buffalo. I was getting married that summer, and as I drove, I wondered, "Should I have gone? Is it going to be worth it?" I had always wanted to play my whole career in Buffalo and retire there, but that wasn't going to happen.

14

TELEVISION MAN

It's been a busy four-plus years since I was traded to the Ottawa Senators early in 2003. Let me tell you about some of the highlights.

The day after I got to Ottawa, I went to the rink and handled all the hoopla, such as interviews with the media, at the morning skate. Then I rolled in for the game and put on the jersey. It felt strange, but at least the colors were similar to the ones the Sabres used. I was never as afraid in my life as I was that night just going out on the ice. I was so nervous I could hardly skate. Once the game got going, I was OK, but it was tough beforehand.

We won the Presidents' Trophy and the first two rounds of the playoffs, and New Jersey was waiting in the Eastern Conference Final. The Devils won three of the first four games, but we won Game Five at home and Game Six in New Jersey. That set up Game Seven back in Ottawa, a game either team could have won. We went out for the first period, and the Devils had nothing. They weren't even in the game. We could have easily taken over the game, but we didn't.

The longer New Jersey stayed in the game, the better it was for them. It came down to a one-goal game at the end, and they got it.

A mistake knocked us out. Wade Redden had a guy coming back into our zone, and Karel Rachunek came flying across to take him but left his guy, Jeff Friesen, wide open. Nice pass, in all alone, boom, ballgame. It was just a bonehead play, and it cost us a chance to get to the finals.

I couldn't find a good situation in the NHL that summer. I decided to do some remodeling jobs in houses back in Buffalo. Larry Quinn—who came back to the Sabres when Tom Golisano took over the team—approached me and said, "If you're not going to play, there's an opportunity here for you to do something." I appreciated that. He was awesome to me. He later asked me if I was interested in doing some TV work with Danny Gare. I'd still be in the game, but I didn't have to travel, and we'd do it all from Buffalo. I took the job.

Danny and I were supposed to work together on segments between periods. I had no idea what that was going to be like because I had never done anything like it before. Before I knew it, the season started that October, I was sitting on a chair, someone counted down, "3 ... 2 ... 1 ...," and I was on the air.

That was a little scary, but Danny was great as a partner. The longer we worked together, the more fun we had. We were comfortable with each other and planned out the segments beforehand, and I think it showed. On road games we'd be back in Buffalo watching on television, and then we'd do our bit on the air. We spent an awful lot of time together in those few months. You get to know somebody pretty quickly that way.

Around the time I started on TV, Quinn called me and said the Sabres wanted to have a "night" honoring me. I told him I hadn't officially retired, but he said he just wanted to have a night of appreciation. I said fine.

That was a pretty nice gesture for someone who was surprised to even get drafted by an NHL team. There are a lot of guys who played longer than I did who never had that recognition. I guess it showed that I gained the respect of the people in Buffalo. What I did was appreciated, and that's nice to know.

When October 28, appreciation night, arrived, I thought someone would say, "How are you doing? Thanks for everything, and see you later." But it was a really nice time. The Sabres invited my mom and dad and my sister's family for it. They came out with a beautiful boat for me. I had no idea that was coming. I told the crowd that if I had known I would get a boat, I would have quit a while ago. When the ceremony was over, I thought to myself, "That's the end. That page of my life is over."

I heard from Doug Gilmour a couple of weeks after that. He said, "You got a boat? They didn't even give my wife roses!" I think instead a donation was made to a charity in Doug's name.

I kept busy that winter, what with the remodeling work, television, and other appearances. Then in January of 2004, the Senators called and asked whether I was interested in coming back to the team for the stretch run and the playoffs. Quinn was the first person I called. "Look, Larry, I have an opportunity to go play. What should I do?" I asked. I didn't say where. He said, "Go. This will be here for you when you come back." Then I told him the whole situation, and he said, "You've got to go." He was awesome that way. I didn't want to make it look like I was running out on him, but I'd kick myself if I had a chance to go and play for Ottawa and the Senators won the Cup without me. He understood.

I officially signed in February, so I guess it wasn't quite time to turn the page after all. I went down to the minors for a week to get a few games in before joining the Senators. It was good to go back to the minors, look at the kids, and see the game in a different way. A lot of the guys down there are trying to make it to the NHL. The kids had a million questions about what the NHL was all about, what it was like, and so on. There were older guys there too who were just trying to hang on to a paycheck, bouncing from place to place and team to team. The first time I was in the minors, I was the young kid. This time, I was the old guy who heard all the questions.

Once I got back to Ottawa, we played Buffalo twice during the rest of the regular season—first time in Ottawa, second time in Buffalo. That was very weird. The Sabres were battling for a playoff spot, and I wanted them to do well ... but not at our expense. We whipped them pretty good, 7–1 in Ottawa. I even got into a fight with Andrew Peters. In my eyes, the game was over, but I think he was more or less pushed to go do something. And I was the person in the way.

We came back to Buffalo in early March, and that was one of the oddest games of my career. The atmosphere beforehand was more like a pick-up game or something. Everyone was talking to everyone. Once I got out there, though, there was no doubt it was an actual game. I was obviously glad to be back, but I didn't even notice the reception I got from the fans. I'm told it was very warm. Heck, my nerves were going, and I wasn't in 100 percent shape. What's more, they put it to us pretty good that night, beating us by the score of 4–3.

I only played in six games for Ottawa in the regular season. In the last one, on March 27 in Toronto, I scored my last goal—number 41 of my career—against Ed Belfour.

The Senators went against Toronto in the playoffs that year, and the series went to a seventh game. Goalie Patty Lalime struggled in that game, and we lost. It was just like the year before, when we lost to New Jersey. If we had gotten by that stumbling block, we might have won it all.

I never played another game in the NHL. The lockout came along in the fall of 2004, and the entire season was cancelled. I had sat out part of the previous year, so I knew what it was like not to go to the rink every day, which made the time away a lot easier for me. During the lockout, I started a little construction company that built and refurbished houses. It kept me busy.

When the two sides reached an agreement, the league announced several rule changes designed to speed the game up. Between those moves and the salary cap, I figured older guys (like me) would be forced out of the game, which is exactly what happened.

When hockey returned in the fall of 2005, I went back to work as one of the Sabres' broadcasters. I think my only fear about the job at that point was about how I would be accepted around the dressing room and the organization. But everyone was great—very supportive. I've never felt uncomfortable.

Kevin Sylvester, Mike Robitaille, and I have developed a good working relationship on the air when we work between periods. It's part of the job to be a little critical of the team and its players when the situation calls for it. I want to believe the guys don't care as long as I'm honest. I also try to back a negative comment up with positives. Too many times, the media will find the negative side to someone's play and run with it. But there's another side to it. Hopefully, players respect me for that.

Sometimes a positive comment can go a long way. The players do listen. They know exactly what's written and said. If they don't know, their wives and friends know, and they'll hear about it. I've had players come up to me and say, "Thanks for what you said." If you show respect, you'll get it back.

The Sabres adapted very well to the new rules. The game is obviously faster, and there are more scoring opportunities. I don't like the way the physical side is nonexistent some nights. Fighting is now a bad thing. If people understood the game more, they'd know what it did for the game. But the fans in Buffalo have accepted the way the game is played now, because the Sabres have played well. It's a team made for the new style.

But if the team wasn't doing so well, the fans might not like it so much. Some nights I watch games involving other teams and say, "This is boring, boring, boring." I don't want to watch power plays all night, and that's what the game is like sometimes. Too many guys now shy away from hits. They don't want to finish their checks. They don't want to go in the corner. Well, that's not the way the game is supposed to be played. You're supposed to give everything you have out there.

Coming out of the lockout, the Sabres had a vision of a direction they wanted to go, with younger guys and speed, but they got lucky too. A lot of guys stepped up and played great hockey. That comes with good scouting. The 2005-06 team might have gone all the way had it not been for several injuries to their defensemen in the playoffs, and they lost to Carolina in the seventh game of the conference final.

The Sabres didn't show any signs of a hangover the following season. They got off to a great start. The young guys didn't know they were supposed to have a letdown. They had confidence because they had won before, and the whole team played well from the start of the regular season to the finish and won the Presidents' Trophy. The Sabres had a few bad weeks, but no real slumps.

Out of 82 regular-season games, the one that will be remembered is the one at home against Ottawa on February 22. That's when

Chris Neil of the Senators gave Chris Drury of the Sabres a concussion with a hit. It was a borderline play. I think Neil could have pulled up. He didn't have to hit him the way he did. Drury was caught watching the play. An injury can happen on a play like that, and Neil should have realized it. A brawl started after the next faceoff that involved everyone on the ice, including the goalies.

I was sitting in the box between the players' benches. That was the very first night that my microphone was live for the whole game. When I had wanted to say something before that, I'd push a button and let the director know I was ready.

After the brawl, there was a lot of yelling from both benches. Then Bryan Murray, the Senators' coach, jumped up on the bench and started yelling at Lindy Ruff, the Sabres coach. Lindy was busy yelling at the refs, and he didn't notice Murray. Bryan made a gesture to me like, "No one is paying attention to me." So I screamed at the top of my head, "Lindy!" I made a gesture for him to look at Murray. Lindy jumped up on the door to the Sabres bench, and the two coaches screamed at each other. It got funny after a while. It went past the point of yelling about the hit to some personal jabs.

The camera caught the two of them at it, with me right in the middle. Rick Jeanneret, our play-by-play announcer, yelled in my ear, "Cover the mike! Cover the mike!" I thought, "Shut the mike off!"

It showed how much hockey means to everyone. It's a fast, emotional game. Things can change in an instant, and you never know when it will happen. The screaming ended when the door that Lindy was standing on blew open. He came crumbling down, and he hurt his shin pretty badly.

Many people have asked me about that night. Oddly, it was an incident that helped both teams. It made the Sabres pull together and show they'd stick up for each other. They handled the situation well. Ottawa's team didn't have an identity before that, and that situation drew them together.

The Sabres of 2006-07 had a whole season of excitement. Buffalo hadn't had a team like that for a long time. Every night, home and away, they had a chance to win. People expected something good to happen, and usually it did. That was fine in the regular season, but the attitude was a little different in the playoffs. Fans expected the Sabres to beat the Islanders and Rangers, and they were looking too far ahead to concentrate on what was directly in front of them.

I don't think the Sabres played well from the beginning of the playoffs. Maybe they underestimated the Islanders and didn't raise their level of intensity. Things came easily to the Sabres all year, so they never had to get in a groove and buckle down. They never had to win a key game. When it came to the playoffs, when they needed to do that, they couldn't make the transition. Meanwhile, Ottawa struggled early in the year. Nothing came easily. Finally, the Senators figured out how to win. There's no switch in hockey to turn on and off, and sometimes the Sabres weren't ready to play desperate hockey.

In the end, I think the Sabres missed Mike Grier, J.P. Dumont, and Jay McKee, who all left in 2006. While some of the regular-season games between the Sabres and Senators were wide open, the playoff series didn't have a freewheeling style. Grier is a tough player. Dumont will go to the front of the net on the power play and take hits in order to score. McKee is a shot blocker who's not afraid to push people around. All three of those guys played a similar style—they weren't flashy, but had more of a playoff style. The Sabres needed that grit against the Senators.

When Game Five of that series was over and the Sabres were eliminated, changes were on the way. There always are, with free agency and trades. Buffalo has plenty of good young players, and more probably are coming, so the Sabres should be fine. Still, it's difficult to see veterans leave. The days when guys will stay 15 years with one team are mostly over. If you're good, somebody will pay you, and that creates movement.

But there are exceptions—like me. It's been almost 20 years since I first came to Buffalo, and it's been great. Players always wonder if they'll be forgotten when they are done with their careers. Thank God that hasn't happened to me. People still want me around, and that's cool. I've tried to give something back when I've had the chance. They say what goes around, comes around, and I believe it.

In Buffalo, it doesn't matter what you do, what you look like, what you drive, what you wear, or how much money you have here. Everybody is the same. I know guys who are multimillionaires and guys who make nothing. But we're all friends, and we do things together.

My wife is from Buffalo, my daughter was born here too. My friends are here. My life revolves around this city. It's a great place to work and raise a family.

Where else would I go? This is home.

ACKNOWLEDGMENTS

The authors wish to thank the following people:

- Tom Borrelli, Greg Connors, and Jody Bailey for reading the manuscript and making several improvements.

- Howard Smith and Steve Jones of *The Buffalo News,* for allowing us to work together, and *The News* for its archives to check facts.

- Harry Scull Jr. for his photographs, and Craig Rybczynski of the Rochester Americans for a photo of Rob during his minor league days.

- Scott Rauguth, Noah Amstadter, and Doug Hoepker of Sports Publishing for encouragement throughout the publishing process.

- A long list of others for their support, ideas, and inspiration, some of whom never dreamed they would see their names in a hockey book: David Abernethy, Donna Andersen, Sean Branagan, Robin Brown, Helen Burggraf, Vickie Carr, Vic Carucci, Tom Coffey, Jim Donathen, Dave Elibol, Irwin Fisch, Bruce Hackett, Claudia Hutton, Jim Kelley, Annette Licitra, Howard Mansfield, Maura McEnaney, Sy Montgomery, Jim Naughton, Kathye Fetsko Petrie, Larry Petry, Randy Schultz, Carol McCormick Semple, Cheryl Solimini, Mike Stanton, Joel Stashenko, Chuck Stevens, Bob Ward, Debbie Ward, and Tim Wendel.